Planning and Managing
Public Relations
Campaigns

PR in Practice Series

**Published in association with the Chartered Institute of Public Relations
Series Editor: Professor Anne Gregory**

Kogan Page has joined forces with the Chartered Institute of Public Relations to publish this unique series which is designed specifically to meet the needs of the increasing numbers of people seeking to enter the public relations profession and the large band of existing PR professionals. Taking a practical, action-oriented approach, the books in the series concentrate on the day-to-day issues of public relations practice and management rather than academic history. They provide ideal primers for all those on CIPR, CAM and CIM courses or those taking NVQs in PR. For PR practitioners, they provide useful refreshers and ensure that their knowledge and skills are kept up to date.

Professor Anne Gregory PhD is Pro Vice Chancellor and Director of the Centre for Public Relations Studies at Leeds Business School, a Faculty of Leeds Metropolitan University. Before entering academic life in 1991 she spent 10 years in public relations at a senior level both in-house and in consultancy, ending her practitioner career as a Board member of a large UK consultancy. At Leeds Metropolitan University Anne oversaw the growth of the public relations area into the largest department in Europe and now is the only full-time professor of Public Relations in the United Kingdom. As Director of the Centre for Public Relations Studies she is responsible for major research and consultancy projects. The Centre's client list includes the UK Cabinet Office, Department of Health, NHS, Local Government Communications, Nokia and Tesco Corporate. She is also a non-executive director of South West Yorkshire Partnership NHS Trust. Anne is Consultant Editor of the PR in Practice series, edited the book of the same name and wrote *Planning and Managing a Public Relations Campaign*, also in this series. She was President of the CIPR in 2004.

Other titles in the series:

Creativity in Public Relations by Andy Green
Effective Internal Communication by Lyn Smith with Pamela Mounter
Effective Media Relations by Michael Bland, Alison Theaker and David Wragg
Effective Personal Communications Skills for Public Relations by Andy Green
Effective Writing Skills for Public Relations by John Foster
Ethics in Public Relations by Patricia J Parsons
Evaluating Public Relations by Tom Watson and Paul Noble
Managing Activism by Denise Deegan
Online Public Relations by David Phillips and Philip Young
Planning and Managing Public Relations Campaigns by Anne Gregory
Public Affairs in Practice by Stuart Thomson and Steve John
Public Relations in Practice edited by Anne Gregory
Public Relations Strategy by Sandra Oliver
Public Relations: A practical guide to the basics by Philip Henslowe
Risk Issues and Crisis Management in Public Relations by Michael Regester and Judy Larkin
Running a Public Relations Department by Mike Beard

The above titles are available from all good bookshops and from the CIPR website www.cipr.co.uk/books. To obtain further information, please contact the publishers at the address below:

Kogan Page Ltd
120 Pentonville Road
London N1 9JN
Tel: 020 7278 0433 Fax: 020 7837 6348
www.koganpage.com

Planning and Managing Public Relations Campaigns

A Strategic Approach

Third Edition

Anne Gregory

CIPR

KoganPage

LONDON PHILADELPHIA NEW DELHI

To those I love and those who love me.

First published as *Planning and Managing a Public Relations Campaign* in Great Britain and the United States in 1996 by Kogan Page Limited
Second edition published as *Planning and Managing Public Relations Campaigns* by Kogan Page, 2000
Third edition 2010

120 Pentonville Road	525 South 4th Street, #241	4737/23 Ansari Road
London N1 9JN	Philadelphia PA 19147	Daryaganj
United Kingdom	USA	New Delhi 110002
www.koganpage.com		India

© Anne Gregory, 1996, 2000, 2010

The right of Anne Gregory to be identified as the author of this work has been asserted by her in accordance with the Copyright, Designs and Patents Act 1988.

ISBN   978 0 7494 5108 0
E-ISBN 978 0 7494 5928 4

British Library Cataloguing-in-Publication Data

A CIP record for this book is available from the British Library.

Library of Congress Cataloging-in-Publication Data

Gregory, Anne, 1953–
    Planning and managing public relations campaigns : a strategic approach / Anne gregory. -- 3rd ed.
        p. c.m.
    Includes index.
    ISBN 978-0-7494-5108-0 -- ISBN 978-0-7494-5928-4 1. Public relations--Management. 2. Public relations--Great Britain. I. Title.
    HD59.G686 2010
    659.2--dc22

                                                                                          2010002521

Typeset by Jean Cussons Typesetting, Diss, Norfolk
Printed and bound in India by Replika Press Pvt Ltd

Contents

Acknowledgements   *ix*
About the author   *xi*

1. Planning and managing: the context   **1**
What is the point of planning?   2
The role of public relations in organizations   5
The role of the public relations professional within organizations   6
The position of public relations within organizations   11
Organizing for action   16
Who does what in public relations?   18

2. Public relations in context   **22**
Context is vitally important   22
Stakeholders and publics   23
Sectoral considerations   26
Organizational development – business stage   27
Organizational characteristics   30
Issues   31
Public opinion   32
Timescales   33
Resources   34

3. **Starting the planning process**   35
    Responsibilities of practitioners   35
    Public relations policy   36
    Why planning is important   38
    Basic questions in planning   39
    The 12 stages of planning   41
    Linking programme planning to the bigger picture   44

4. **Research and analysis**   47
    Embedding research in the planning process   47
    The first planning step   50
    Analysing the environment   51
    Analysing the organization   57
    Analysing the stakeholder   59
    Who should undertake the research?   61
    Research techniques   62
    Investment in research pays – two cases in point   69

5. **Communication theory and setting aims and objectives**   76
    Knowing where you're going   76
    Attitude is all important   77
    The communication chain   78
    How 'receivers' use information   86
    Setting realistic aims and objectives   89
    Golden rules of objective setting   92
    Constraints on aims and objectives   94
    Different levels of aims and objectives   95

6. **Knowing the publics and messages**   97
    Who shall we talk to and what shall we say?   97
    What is public opinion?   99
    Types of publics   100
    Using other segmentation techniques   104
    So what about the media?   106
    The implications for targeting publics   107
    How to prioritize publics   107
    What shall we say?   109
    Constructing the content   110
    Crafting messages   114
    How the message should be presented   115

7. **Strategy and tactics**   **117**
    Getting the strategy right   117
    What is strategy?   118
    From strategy to tactics   118
    What tactics should be employed?   120
    Different campaigns need different tactics   125
    Sustaining long-term programmes   131
    Contingency and risk planning   134

8. **Timescales and resources**   **138**
    Timescales   138
    Task planning techniques   139
    Critical path analysis   141
    Longer-term plans   143
    Resources   149

9. **Knowing what has been achieved: evaluation and review**   **156**
    Measuring success   156
    The benefits of evaluation   157
    Why practitioners don't evaluate   158
    Principles of evaluation   160
    Evaluation terminology   161
    Levels of evaluation   163
    A programme evaluation model and some other measures   164
    Media analysis   172
    Reviewing the situation   174
    And finally   178

Index   *179*

Free online support material can be downloaded from the
Kogan Page website. Please go to:
www.koganpage.com/PlanningAndManagingPublicRelations
Campaigns

Acknowledgements

In drawing up a list of those organizations and individuals who must be thanked for helping with the writing of this book, it is very difficult to know where to start.

First of all there are all the organizations I have worked for and with whom over the years I have built up my knowledge and experience of public relations to an extent where this book was possible.

Then there are those who have generously supplied me with materials, including the Chartered Institute of Public Relations (I have borrowed shamelessly from their Excellence Awards), Pilkington PLC, Lansons Communications, Echo Research, Edelman, Trimedia, The Cabinet Office, Stockport and Norfolk County Council and The Worshipful Company of World Traders.

I would like to thank the public relations students at Leeds Metropolitan University and those working professionals for whom I prepare materials on planning and managing public relations, and who constantly stimulate my thinking.

I am very grateful to Ben Cotton who helped me with the case studies and Rosie Boston, my fantastic PA, who did the final word-processing for me and supported me throughout the process.

To the CIPR/Kogan Page Editorial Board, many thanks for your encouragement and support.

About the author

Professor Anne Gregory PhD is Pro Vice Chancellor and Director of the Centre for Public Relations Studies at Leeds Business School, a Faculty of Leeds Metropolitan University.

Before entering academic life in 1991 she spent 10 years in public relations at a senior level both in-house and in consultancy, ending her practitioner career as a Board member of a large UK consultancy.

At Leeds Metropolitan University Anne oversaw the growth of the public relations area into the largest department in Europe and now is the only full-time professor of Public Relations in the United Kingdom. As Director of the Centre for Public Relations Studies she is responsible for major research and consultancy projects. The Centre's client list includes the UK Cabinet Office, Department of Health, NHS, Local Government Communications, Nokia and Tesco Corporate. She is also a non-executive director of South West Yorkshire Partnership NHS Trust.

She was President of the Chartered Institute of Public Relations in 2004 and led it to Chartered status. She initiated the CIPR/Kogan Page series of books on public relations and is its consultant editor.

Anne is an academic and strategic adviser to practice of international standing. She is widely published in books and leading journals and is involved in international research and consultancy aimed at raising the standards of practice in the profession.

1

Planning and managing: the context

The world of public relations has changed radically in the last few years. Indeed, as a barometer of society itself, it has had to. The challenges we face as a society, such as globalization, global warming, the need to re-base our notions of business and to re-evaluate our values away from ever increasing consumption, are unparalleled.

Added to that are the seismic changes that new, communications-based technologies bring to the way we connect and the nature of the interactions we have. These changes are generating fundamental shifts in power away from traditional sources of authority. Those individuals and groups who can understand what is going on and are able to work with the new communication tools at our disposal will emerge as a new elite.

It is not the remit of this book to explore the details and ramifications of all these deep and wide changes that are happening, but the impact on the practice of public relations overall is profound and therefore cannot be ignored. A report by the Arthur W Page Society in 2007 called *The Authentic Enterprise*[1], examines and evaluates some of these issues and concludes that we have reached a point of 'strategic inflection' which requires organizations to embrace a new way of operating: communication is at the heart and the key is authenticity. It goes on to enumerate four new practices and skills for which the more senior public relations practitioner must assume a leadership role:

- defining and instilling company values;
- building and managing multi-stakeholder relationships;
- enabling the enterprise with 'new media' skills and tools;
- building and managing trust in all its dimensions.

This view is very much complemented by the findings of the European Communication Monitor 2009[2], which reveals that senior corporate communicators believe that by 2012 they will have increased their activity in responsible business and sustainability, internal communication and change management, international communication, and coaching and training in public relations and communication skills. Conversely the proportion of time spent on marketing/consumer public relations, traditional media relations and investor relations will have decreased.

Organizations will have to be adept at responding to a variety of societal issues, they will have to engage with a range of stakeholders who to date have not been on their radar and who will hold them to account in new ways and they will need to engage in different ways. They will have to demonstrate that they are living their espoused values and the mandate, or 'licence to operate', given them by this complex web of multi-stakeholders will be fragile and in need of attention and reinforcement constantly. Their organizations will be judged not only by their corporate words and actions, but by the myriad of individual transactions that they and their employees engage in – hence the increased emphasis on internal communication and coaching.

WHAT IS THE POINT OF PLANNING?

It is quite legitimate to ask, therefore, given the level of complexity that public relations practitioners face and the fact that things are in constant flux and change, what is the point of planning and managing public relations programmes at all? Undoubtedly there are individual communicators who thrive in chaos, who 'sense' their way through situations and are very good at it. Most people are not like that, they are rational creatures who seek a level of order and who, as far as possible, want to be able to operate in a work environment that has some control and predictability about it. Having a sense of direction and of what is important is part of wellbeing at work and indeed, management by objectives is an accepted way to frame and prioritize work.

Furthermore, organizations are purposeful entities. They exist for a reason, whether that is to fulfil a social or business purpose. They too are mainly based on rational and tested business models that comprise recognized working principles and established methods of planning. These can vary enormously between those organizations that employ quite mechanistic processes and bureaucratic planning approaches, to those who are more entrepreneurial and intuitive in their planning, but who are nonetheless strict in identifying and evaluating business opportunities and ensuring that new ventures are in line with what the brand stands for.

Public relations as a functional department of any organization needs to follow the same disciplines that other functional departments such as legal, finance, HR and operations do if it is to be respected and if its activities are to properly support and shape the organization. A key feature of the strategic role of public relations (which will be explored in this book) is that it is founded on a clear understanding of the contribution that the function can make and an underpinning philosophy and way of operating that are research-informed. Tactical public relations on the other hand focuses on the delivery of communication services as directed by others.

Strategic planning does not mean that everything can be controlled: that is never possible, but it does take the planner through a process that helps them define the contribution they can make, how they can go about their tasks and how they are to measure if they have been successful. They must be mindful that a level of flexibility and pragmatic adjustment is required along the way, and indeed unforeseen events may require a radical departure from even the best of plans. Planning and managing strategic programmes is both scientific and creative. It is a process that stimulates the intellect, engages the emotions and puts the building blocks in place for creating efficient and effective interventions for the planner's organization.

A starting point

A starting point when conducting strategic public relations planning is to examine some of the definitions. According to the UK Chartered Institute of Public Relations (CIPR), which is Europe's largest professional body in the field:

> Public relations is the discipline which looks after reputation, with the aim of earning understanding and support and influencing opinion and behaviour. It is the planned and sustained effort to establish and maintain goodwill and mutual understanding between an organization and its publics.

At the heart of this definition is the notion that public relations has to be planned. It is a deliberate, carefully thought-through process. It also requires ongoing (sustained) activity: it is not haphazard. The activity is concerned with initiating (establishing) and maintaining a process of mutual understanding. In other words it involves a dialogue where an organization and its various publics seek to listen to each other and understand each other. This will usually result in some change or action by the parties involved. Note, the change can be both ways.

The first part of this definition covers the idea of reputation. A good reputation is not something that is earned overnight. It has to be carefully and considerately cultivated. It is something that is earned over a period of time as understanding and support develop for an organization. The development of reputation has to be meticulously undertaken with integrity and honesty and because reputation is a notion that exists in the perceiver's mind (like image) this is a complex process. It is also something that is very fragile and can be lost quickly if words or actions are found to be out of step with reality, or if rumour gets out of hand. There is no better example of that than Nike, who despite their statements on ethical business were exposed as exploiting child labour.

On the other hand the careful handling by Apple and fresh fruit drinks producer Innocent of their reputations means that they have enjoyed public esteem for many years. The reality of their spoken, public claims is borne out by their actual products and services.

A virtuous circle is created where a good reputation raises expectations about the kind of products or services a company supplies and the quality of the products or services enhances reputation.

Public relations has a major contribution to make

All this means that public relations has a significant contribution to make. It can contribute directly to organizational success. If its task is guarding and managing reputation and relationships this must have a demonstrable effect, and not just result in a 'feelgood' factor. Spending money on establishing a dialogue with key publics and building a reputation does result in tangible benefits to the organization. Publics are influenced in their favour.

If a company has a good reputation the evidence is that people are more likely to:

- try its new products;
- buy its shares;
- believe its advertising;
- want to work for it;
- do business with it when all other things are equal;
- support it in difficult times;
- give it a higher financial value.

For private sector companies these benefits often become apparent when the organization is sold. The actual fixed asset value of a company will be declared, but on top of that a buyer will pay a premium for goodwill or the good name of the company – its brand. That is when an actual value is put on the reputation of the company and reputations are built by developing strong and valuable relationships with stakeholders who count. Establishing and maintaining a good reputation with key publics is a meticulous, time- and energy-consuming business, requiring all the skills and attributes of planners and managers of the highest calibre.

THE ROLE OF PUBLIC RELATIONS
IN ORGANIZATIONS

To understand how public relations programmes and campaigns are planned and managed, it is first essential to understand the role of public relations in organizations.

It is not the aim of this book to go into the detail of how organizations are structured and managed, and how they function. There are many excellent textbooks on this. It is, however, incumbent on all public relations practitioners to understand these issues; otherwise they will not be able to fulfil their proper role within their organization and certainly will not be able to operate as senior managers.

Simply put, an organization consists of three elements:

- fixed assets such as its buildings, office furniture, car fleet and products;
- liquid assets or the money which lubricates the business;
- people.

Its fixed assets have a finite value and can be accounted for on a balance sheet. Similarly, the amount of liquid assets an organization has can be measured. It is obvious that the number of people that work for an organization can be counted, but in many ways employees are an unquantifiable asset. Their capabilities are basically unbounded. They are the ones who put life into an organization to create added value. They are the ones who use their creativity and ingenuity to design new products and sell them. They provide the customer service. They make organizations work.

Furthermore, people interact with other people who are not necessarily a formal part of the organization. They create customer relationships, they have families and friends who may or who may not support their organization. They deal with suppliers, with local and central government, with the local community and so on.

People are an infinitely expandable resource and they blur the edges of an organization's boundaries by drawing into the organization other people, who strictly speaking are external to its operation. Furthermore, some employees are also members of groups external to the organization, but critical to its success. As well as being employees, they can be customers, shareholders, and are probably members of the local community.

In addition, employees are virtually connected. They blog, are members of social networks and online communities, they twitter and have an almost infinite variety of potential connections at their disposal.

In times past, the public relations department was the formal conduit for internal and external communications. Of course there was always a flourishing grapevine of informal communication internally and externally, but the limitations of technology, or the requirement to meet face to face, meant that this was largely bounded in time and reach. Now there is no such barrier. Everyone has the potential to be a powerful channel of communication and can create their own content with ease. Thus organizational boundaries become ever more porous… information can leak out from any source. In addition, organizations are also more transparent: people from outside can look in very easily and connect with a range of individuals to build up their own picture of the organization. If that picture is different from the one presented in formal channels, there is a potential issue for the organization. This level of interconnectedness provides therefore, a very permeable organization, linked to a host of formal and informal stakeholders through a host of formal and informal channels. Figure 1.1 illustrates some of that complexity, but it by no means captures all the stakeholder groups, channels or interactions that happen between an organization and stakeholders.

The main role of the chief executive of an organization is to provide vision. That vision will give direction to the organization: a picture of the future that can be arrived at and organized for. Badly managed organizations have no clear direction, but stumble along being constantly diverted to deal with the crises or apparent opportunities of the day without being focused on achieving their main, long-term objectives.

THE ROLE OF THE PUBLIC RELATIONS PROFESSIONAL WITHIN ORGANIZATIONS

An organization's strategy (which determines how the vision will be realized) is determined after a great deal of analysis and decision making. Analysis of how chief executives go about this reveals that it is often conversation based. Ideas are advanced and tested and revised, rejected or re-ordered. Out of this iterative process a route map to the realization of the vision is developed. Many people, both outside and inside the organization, will contribute to this process. Having developed a strategy, this will

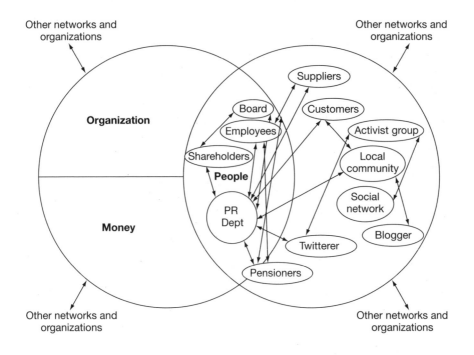

Figure 1.1   *The multi-stakeholder, multi-connected view of organizational structure*

need to be communicated so that it can be supported and implemented. Public relations has an essential role to play in this process, both in helping to develop the strategy itself and in its communication.

Relationships provide intelligence

The job of the public relations professional is to communicate with and build relationships with all the organization's publics. They are (or should be) acutely aware of the environment in which the organization operates. This is vital because publics exist within that environment and it is not possible to understand people fully unless there is a clear appreciation of the social, technological, economic, political and cultural issues and factors that influence them and drive their lives. Being in touch with the public mood, having contextual intelligence is essential. Organizations that are not conscious of the public mood find themselves in difficulties, whereas those in touch with it can find that it provides a significant advantage. Thus the Walmart-owned supermarket chain Asda stopped using celebrity models for its George range of clothing in 2009 because its Pulse of the Nation research told it that the excesses of the celebrity lifestyle clashed with

7

the experience of their customers, many of whom were facing the harsh realities of the recession. Instead they used 'ordinary' people, representative of their customer base. Public relations professionals, along with other colleagues, can supply that contextual intelligence to decison-making planners. Thus they can be seen to have a 'boundary-spanning' role. They operate at the edge of the organization, bridging the gap between it and its external publics. They have one foot in the organization and one foot outside. Being able to represent the views of externalpublics, and their likely reactions to decisions, is a vital perspective that public relations professionals can bring to strategic planning. Furthermore, public relations professionals are also usually the communication managers within organizations and can draw information together about an organization's internal publics. The issues and concerns of external publics may well be reflected internally, but there will also be additional issues and concerns that affect employees as members of the organization.

Information about the specifics of contextual factors, for example economic and financial facts, and intelligence about public opinion generally, will also be provided by specialists scattered throughout the organization. The public relations function, because of its 'boundary-spanning role', can act as a central intelligence-gathering function and, provided there are suitably trained individuals, supply an analysis and interpretation service too.

This strategic use of the public relations function implies that there is a recognition of its status by management. Public relations is more than a tactical tool used purely to 'communicate' information or add a gloss to information. It is an integral part of the strategic development process grounded on thorough-going research and skilled, objective analysis.

Some of the linkages that the public relations function have are invaluable sources of early information and can pinpoint emerging issues that may have profound impact on an organization. For example, monitoring of the blogosphere or of Twitter traffic can help to identify emerging 'hot' issues. Media content analysis can identify the importance of an issue or the direction that public opinion is likely to take on an issue. Public affairs contacts can flag up government thinking on prospective legislation and think tanks can give opinions on likely social or economic change.

Being able to make sense of the environment, public relations professionals not only provide intelligence to the strategic development process, but contribute to the general decision making within organizations. Furthermore, because they have antennae that are alert to the external and internal environment that the organization operates within, they can bring an invaluable, independent perspective to decision making by managers' who are often too close to a situation to act objectively, or who are unaware of some of the ramifications of those decisions as far as the wider world is concerned. It could well be that what on the face of it appears to be correct business decisions have to be questioned when they are set within a broader, stakeholder context. For example, it might make apparent business sense for an organization to obtain supplies from the cheapest, most reliable source. But what if that source is thousands of miles away and the environmental impact of transporting these supplies is considerable?

There is therefore a twofold role for the public relations professional here. First, it is to keep senior management informed of what is happening in the social environment, which is peopled by its stakeholders, so that this is taken into account as decisions are made. The communication process is two-way as Figure 1.2 shows.

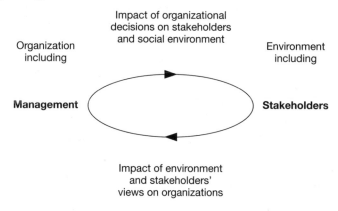

Figure 1.2   *The two-way information flow between an organization and its environment*

Second, it is to counsel management on the implications of its decisions, taking into account the likely reaction of key publics who directly affect the well-being or otherwise of a company. The public relations professional is the monitor of public opinion, and the conscience and ethical mentor of the organization.

Communication skill

Once strategy is determined, it needs to be communicated. Ideally, during the process of strategic development, external and internal stakeholders will have been involved. The organization will have tested various propositions and have asked for the input of employees and other stakeholders. So, again, ideally there will be no surprises, and through the process of prior discussion and engagement stakeholders will already be amenable to the final version. Technology-driven tools make this type of consultation relatively easy and the benefits of building up a web of influence and positive relationships are obvious. The converse is deeply undesirable. Public relations professionals can be used by senior management to advise on both the content of the communication itself and the mechanics to be used for relaying the content to publics and back from them. Because strategic information and plans are so important, management are often tempted to communicate them in technical and/or pompous language and in an inappropriate form, for example a highly glossy brochure that permits no discussion or feedback. The information is presented as a 'done deal'. The communication professional must resist such actions and provide skilled advice on how to undertake the communication task.

The very process of insisting that communication is clear and relevant for the people who will consume it helps to put rigour into strategic thinking and decision making. It helps to eliminate woolly, unrealistic aspirations and forces management to think through the practical implications of their planning. It is possible to cloak reality behind fine-sounding words, but distilling ideas down to clear and relevant language provides a check on how realistic those ideas are and makes comparisons between what's said and what's done more simple. The task of the public relation professional is to check whether the reality meets the claim, and if not, to point this out.

At a tactical level, the role of the public relations practitioner is to manage appropriate communication between an organization and its stakeholders and vice versa by ensuring that both the content and the channel are suitable and timely.

For example, shareholders will want to know about the future development plans of a company in some detail, including its overseas aspirations. How and when that information is relayed to them is very important. UK customers, on the other hand, may be less likely to be so concerned about this. They will want to know that a particular shop will be open next week, or that a favourite product will continue to be available. The fact that the company plans to open outlets in Hong Kong or Singapore in 2014 will probably not concern them, unless of course they are shareholders too, or an activist group with a particular concern about trading in these markets.

The importance of communication

So why is communication important?

First of all it helps to further the strategic objectives of an organization because it is the vehicle used to enlist the support of all the various groups or key publics by ensuring the vision and values of the chief executive and organization are understood. The point of the communication is not just to pass on information about the vision, but to gain active pursuit of or at least assent to those objectives (depending on the public). The communication is designed to influence behaviour.

Of course, if the organization listens as well as speaks and acts, its communication will have been influenced by research undertaken with those key publics as mentioned earlier, but it will also continue to be affected by them as it continues to listen. It is, therefore, more likely to be effective in its communication and action, as it is not likely to say and do things that are opposed by its stakeholders.

Second, it positively fosters relationships with key publics. These publics are ultimately responsible for the destiny of the organization for good or ill. Good communication enhances the opportunities for incremental intelligence providing an 'early warning' system for the organization. In this way it can capitalize on opportunities that are presented to it by both identifying them early and facilitating the actions that are required to capture them (for example, if this is a sales opportunity or an opportunity to influence legislation). It also helps minimize the threats by spotting problems or potential conflicts early (for example, identifying increasing employee disquiet, or discontent with a proposed company action coming from an influential blogger).

THE POSITION OF PUBLIC RELATIONS WITHIN ORGANIZATIONS

More detailed information on the role of public relations practitioners is given in Chapter 2. At this stage it is important to look at the position and status that public relations occupies within organizations, since that is linked to its role as a strategic or tactical function.

A good indication of how public relations is regarded is to establish where the function is placed. It is no surprise that the European Communication Monitor 2009[3] found that the more senior the lead public relations practitioner was in the organization, the more influence they had. If senior public relations managers are part of the 'dominant coalition' of company decision-makers, then public relations is likely to serve a key strategic role. Those individuals are likely to undertake the research and counselling activities already outlined. If not, public relations is likely to be largely tactical. It could well be seen just as a part of the marketing communications mix or regarded as mainly to do with presenting information about the organization in an acceptable (usually to the organization) way.

Another indication of how seriously the activity is taken is to gauge whether it is mainly reactive or proactive. There is always a level of reactive public relations in any organization. However good the planning, the unexpected is likely to occur, whether that be a pressure group making an unexpected attack (justified or ill-founded) or another organization making a takeover bid out of the blue. There are also opportunistic openings that should be grasped. For example, British Airways provided transport for the very successful British Olympic Team to and from the Beijing Olympics in 2008. Because the team won so many medals, overnight BA painted the nosecone of the returning aircraft gold and renamed it 'Pride'. They also hosted a celebratory return at the new Terminal 5 in Heathrow. This quickly organized sequence proved highly beneficial, associating the airline with the successful team and helped to rebuild its reputation following the problems encountered with the opening of Terminal 5.

In organizations where public relations is taken seriously and proactively, it is normally found that the senior practitioner holds a major position in the organization. Apart from being a good all-round business manager with the battery of appropriate skills and knowledge that all managers must have, he or she will provide a counselling role for fellow senior managers and directors and will have overall responsibility for the communication strategy of the organization. That might include determining the key overall marketing, advertising and promotional strategy. It will certainly involve working very closely with those disciplines.

Activity will be directed at building reputation positively and will have a strategic purpose. Issues like social responsibility and corporate governance will be taken seriously. Programmes will be based on careful formal and informal research, and a knowledge of who the key publics are, how these publics regard the organization and what they see as priorities. Communication with publics will be dialogue-based with the organization being responsive, indeed willing to collaborate with these publics. The programmes that are devised will be concerned with impact, and aim to influence attitudes, opinions and behaviours. They will not be obsessed with process such as how many news releases are produced, but the effectiveness of public relations activity will be closely monitored as will the quality of the relationships that are being built. Often these organizations will be industry leaders and set the pace in the market, as research by Gregory and Edwards[4] found with the UK's Most Admired Companies. They will usually be the ones available to the media and seen to be the voice of their industry. They are open, communicative organizations.

In organizations where public relations is seen as a lower order activity and where its practice is normally reactive, certain telltale traits will be evident. The practitioner will not hold a senior management role and will not be involved in decision making. The task will be to respond to events and will often be defensive. The function will tend to communicate what has already happened, and the activity will be largely one-way, with the organization telling the world what it has done or is doing and not being influenced by what the world is saying to it. Any progress will be an evolution of what has happened in the past. The practitioner will not feel valued or in control and will not be a part of the 'dominant coalition'.

It is partly the public relations industry and individual practitioners who have perpetuated this reactive, technical role for public relations. Too often public relations has been regarded as just media relations and recruitment has been largely from the field of journalism where the priority is to 'get the story out'. Public relations is restricted to free media publicity – or as just a part of marketing communication. The schematic in Figure 1.3 shows the relationship between public relations and marketing, and indicates the shared areas of activity and those areas where public relations has a quite separate remit.

Research by Moss and colleagues[5] has found that the main reason why practitioners are not taken seriously as senior organizational players is because they do not know enough about how the sector and the business operates. How can they be at the decision-making table if they have no real grasp on what makes a business tick?

In surveys, lack of financial and budgeting skills are perceived as being the greatest deficiency in public relations practitioners. Other deficiencies are problem solving and decision making, goal setting and prioritising, planning and organization, analytical skills and time management.

To mature fully as a discipline, public relations must take on the responsibilities of knowledge, planning and management just as any other business function.

The contribution of public relations at different levels in the organization

It goes without saying that organizations operate at different levels and it is important to understand these in order to define the contribution that public relations can make at these various levels. There is often confusion about terms like strategy and how it is used; for example, corporate strategy, programme strategy and operational strategy. Being clear about the levels of strategy helps public relations practitioners to talk about their role in a way that is meaningful throughout the organization.

The South African academic Benita Steyn[6] has done a great deal of work on matching the various levels of strategy in business to what she sees to be equivalent level activities undertaken by public relations professionals, however, her work focuses on the private sector. More practitioners work for the not-for-profit or public sector than the private sector. Work supported by the CIPR in the UK (Gregory and White, 2008) has identified that public relations can make a contribution and be measured and evaluated at four levels. Figure 1.4 shows these levels.

In brief, the contribution of public relations at the four levels is as follows:

Societal

Public relations can and does make a contribution to society, particularly by

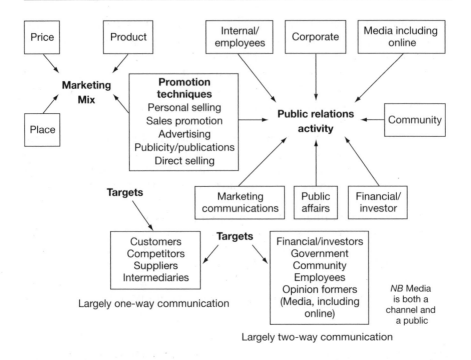

Figure 1.3   *The inter-relationship of public relations and marketing*

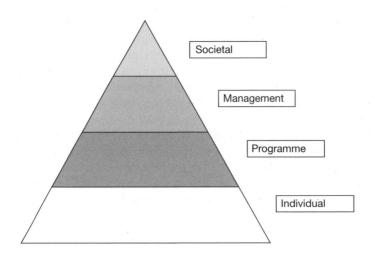

Figure 1.4   *The levels at which public relations can make a contribution[7]*

helping organizations understand their obligations in this direction. Much of this work is around helping organizations define and implement their values so that they maintain support, 'or licence to operate', from the general public. Corporate responsibility commitments are an expression of an organization's societal level strategy.

Management

At this level public relations makes a contribution to management, leadership and organizational performance by helping senior managers make better decisions. These decisions are informed by intelligence gathered from and about stakeholder groups and understanding what stakeholder opinions are on issues. Knowledge about stakeholders' likely reactions to decisions also helps organizations avoid mistakes.

Programme

Planning, designing and implementing communication programmes and activities that will help deliver societal and management level objectives.

The types of specific activities the public relations function will be involved in commonly include (but this is not the complete list):

- Constructing communication programmes and activities to support delivery of organizational priorities.
- Advising management and delivering campaigns of different types depending on the requirements of the stakeholder group involved, for example, social marketing programmes for behaviour change (eg childhood obesity), mass media campaigns for information dissemination (eg changes in the date when tax returns must be made), personalized/ one-to-one engagement (eg with regulators or key delivery partners).
- Using recognized business disciplines to design effective communication plans that also embrace the full range of communication techniques, including social marketing and online.
- Moving seamlessly between reactive, proactive and interactive roles depending on the relationship with the stakeholder involved.
- Evaluating programmes and communication activities for effectiveness.

At this level, a great deal of time is spent on putting together public relations plans of different types depending on the needs of the stakeholder groups involved. Hence, social marketing programmes may be needed to encourage behavioural change in society as a whole, for example, driving more safely; marketing campaigns will be aimed at potential customers to help product sales, lobbying campaigns targeted at MPs individually will be mounted to influence voting intentions and so on.

Each plan will be different depending on its purpose; who is involved; their communication channel-use habits; the timing of the campaign etc. However, the disciplines behind the planning process are the same and it is this that this book is primarily about.

Individual

The performance of individual practitioners in their functional role underpins the first three levels of operating outlined above. An individual's competence and capability is critical to their personal success in their role and in the way public relations as a whole will be perceived in the organization.

The point of going through the strategic levels at which public relations can make a contribution is to:

- clarify the types of input that public relations can make to the organization as a whole, including its input to organizational decision making;
- demonstrate that public relations contributes more to an organization than just programmes and campaigns – it makes a strategic input at all levels;
- show that programmes and campaigns have to be seen within a broader context and ensure all programmes are aligned to societal and management objectives;
- enable the practitioner to articulate and move between the various roles that they must play within the organization.

ORGANIZING FOR ACTION

Another book in this series, *Running a Public Relations Department*, looks in detail at how the public relations function should be organized. However, this is covered briefly here to provide an indication of the main things to be considered.

The way the public relations operation is usually organized is to split it along either task or functional lines. Single operators, however, have to do everything.

Some organizations have a task-oriented structure, that is, tasks requiring particular skills and knowledge are separated out and given to small groups or individuals to perform. Thus the structure may be as follows:

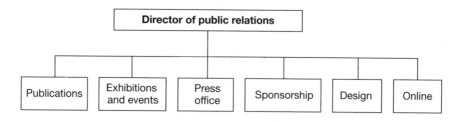

Other organizations split on functional lines. That is, the areas of activity are separated out and groups or individuals tackle all the tasks. A functional structure may look something like this:

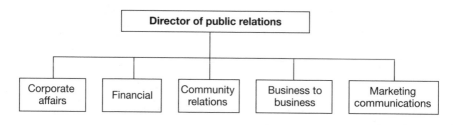

However, in some organizations neither of these structures are employed. The view is that the public relations team effectively operates as an internal consultancy, working on long- or short-term public relations projects that will require a range of tasks and functions to be undertaken. The department is therefore structured in teams depending on the requirements of the project. Any one individual may belong to a number of project teams. Working like this can cut across some of the silo thinking that comes about with task- or functional-based teams. It also means that individuals can work with colleagues with a variety of knowledge and skills, facilitating learning from each other and determining together the best way to approach the project. Teamworking in this way can bring a great deal of variety and job satisfaction, but it also requires good team leadership and management and greater flexibility in the public relations department.

A typical structure in this matrix arrangement, which can appear quite 'messy', might look like the diagram on page 18.

Where public relations is conducted for a company that is split into separate operating companies, sometimes with different names, the situation is infinitely more variable. Some groups have very large corporate departments which undertake activity for the group as a whole and for all the operating companies. In other groups there is a very small corporate operation dealing with major corporate activities such as financial and

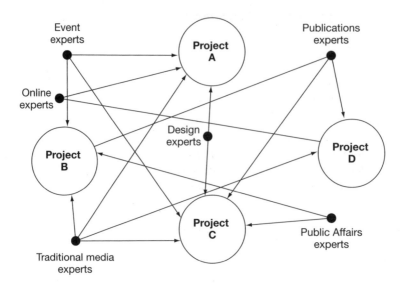

government affairs, and maybe corporate sponsorship. The rest of the activity is then devolved to the operating companies. Normally the operating pattern that applies in the business as a whole also applies to public relations activity, that is, if business is very much driven from the centre then public relations is likely to be located in the centre also. On the other hand, if the approach is to let the operating companies function as virtually autonomous units, then it is also likely that public relations will be devolved to them.

WHO DOES WHAT IN PUBLIC RELATIONS?

Seminal work on public relations roles spearheaded by Glen Broom[8] and David Dozier[9] identified two dominant public relations roles:

- *The communication technician.* Who is not involved in making organizational decisions but who carries out public relations programmes such as writing press releases, editing house magazines and designing web pages. This person is probably not too involved in undertaking research or evaluating programmes; he or she is concerned primarily with implementation.
- *The communication manager.* Who plans and manages public relations programmes, counsels management, makes communication policy decisions and so on.

Within this second category, there are three main types of manager role.

- *The expert prescriber.* Who researches and defines public relations problems, develops programmes and implements them, maybe with the assistance of others.
- *The communication facilitator.* Who acts as a go-between, keeping two-way communication between an organization and its publics. He or she is a liaison person, interpreter and mediator.
- *The problem-solving process facilitator.* Who helps others in the organization solve their public relations problems. This person acts as a sort of counsellor/adviser on the planning and implementation of programmes. (This is a role often fulfilled by specialist consultancies.)

David Dozier also identifies two middle-level roles that sit between the manager and the technician role.

- *Media relations role.* This is a two-way function where the individual keeps the media informed, and informs the organization of the needs and concerns of the media. This is not just the production and dissemination of messages from the organization to the media, but a highly skilled role requiring detailed knowledge and a profound understanding of the media. It is often fulfilled by someone who has made the crossover from journalism to public relations. It also goes some way to explaining why, if a former journalist is employed to undertake public relations, the function remains focused on media relations.
- *Communication and liaison role.* A higher-level public relations role representing the organization at events and meetings, and positively creating opportunities for management to communicate with internal and external publics.

The broad technician and manager roles vary from organization to organization. At the lower level, in large organizations split on task lines, a technician may only write for the house journal. In other organizations he or she may do several other writing jobs too, such as preparing speeches and writing copy for the website, especially if the department is functional in orientation or if it is small.

At the middle level, practitioners may be responsible for a whole press relations programme or undertake employee relations only. They may be involved in both. Some may specialize in research or planning and have little to do with implementation, or they may be an account executive in a consultancy who is responsible for a range of planning and implementation tasks.

At higher levels, public relations managers plan whole programmes and counsel senior management on policy, as well as supervise middle- and lower-level practitioners.

In practice most public relations activities require a mixture of technician and manager roles. Many managers hold a number of the management roles indicated either at the same time, or at various stages in their careers, and not many people, at this stage of the profession's growth, are entirely removed from the implementation role.

Dozier and Broom[10] also identified a 'senior advisor' role at the managerial level: someone who acted as a high-level counsellor, constantly advising the Chief Executive Officer, or Chair of the Board. They have a broad-ranging remit, but are effectively charged with spotting issues or difficulties for the individual they work with and advising them on how to respond.

More recently, Moss, Newman and De Santo[11] reported the findings of empirical work they had undertaken in both the UK and the United States that isolated five elements in the senior public relations role. Four are very much linked to the managerial role: monitor and evaluator (for the whole organization's performance as measured by reputation and relationships, see earlier in this chapter); key policy and strategy advisor; trouble shooter/ problem solver; and issues management expert. They also discovered that even the most senior managers take on some technical work, usually high risk or complex work, such as, for example, dealing with senior people in the financial world on corporate earnings.

In the 2009 survey of Communications Directors mentioned earlier, of those at the most senior level (CEO of a consultancy or Director in an organization), 64 per cent believe that they actually shape organizational strategy as well as supporting business goals, which of course means that over a third do not. All the evidence points to there still being some way to go in establishing senior public relations practitioners as being automatically involved in strategy making.

The growing complexity of the issues that public relations practitioners are being asked to handle is leading to increasing specialization in some areas. At the simplest level this is demonstrated by the fact that many consultancies now bill themselves as specialists in, for example, fashion or celebrity or online public relations and the larger, one-stop agencies have for a long time had quite discrete specialist functions within them, such as public affairs or consumer divisions. Indeed, the evidence is that many now are splitting along technician and senior counsellor lines, with the technical aspects of public relations becoming increasingly commoditized and indeed automated as much as possible, thereby keeping prices down. At the other end of the scale, however, there is a growing requirement for in-house practitioners and consultancies to promote high level advice to the Board and most senior executives of organizations.

Notes

1. A copy of this report can be obtained at www.awpagesociety.com.
2. For a copy of the findings of the Communication Monitor 2009 see www.communicationmonitor.eu/ECM2009-Results-ChartVersion.pdf.
3. See www.communicationmonitor.eu/ECM2009-Results-ChartVersion. pdf.
4. Gregory, A and Edwards, L (2004) Patterns in PR of Britain's Most Admired Companies. Report commissioned by Eloqui Public Relations from The Centre for Public Relations Studies, Leeds Business School, Leeds Metropolitan University.
5. Moss, D A, Newman, A and De Santo, B (2005) What do communication managers do? Defining and refining the core elements of management in a public relations/communication context, *Journalism and Mass Communication Quarterly*, **32**, pp 873–90.
6. Steyn, B (2007) Contribution of Public Relations to Organizational Strategy Formulation, in *The Future of Excellence in Public Relations and Communication Management*, ed, E Toth, Lawrence Erlbaum Associates, Mahwah, NJ.
7. Gregory, A and White, J (2008) Introducing the Chartered Institute of Public Relations Initiative: Moving on from talking about evaluation to incorporating it into better management of the practice, in B Van Ruler, A Tkalac Vercic and D Vercic (eds) *Public Relations Metrics: Research and evaluation*, Routledge, New York.
8. Broom, G M and Smith, G D (1979) Testing the practitioner's impact on clients, *Public Relations Review*, **5**, pp 47–59.
   Broom, G M (1982) A comparison of sex roles in public relations, *Public Relations Review*, **5** (3), pp 17–22.
9. Dozier, D M and Broom, G M (1995) Evolution of the manager role in public relations practice, *Journal of Public Relations Research*, **7** (1), pp 3–26.
10. Dozier, D M and Broom, G M (1995) Evolution of the manager role in public relations practice, *Journal of Public Releations Research*, **7** (1), pp 3–26.
11. Moss, D A, Newman, A and De Santo, B (2005) What do communication managers do? Defining and refining the core elements of management in a public relations/communication context, *Journalism and Mass Communication Quarterly*, **32**, pp 873–90.

2

Public relations in context

CONTEXT IS VITALLY IMPORTANT

To plan and manage programmes (long term, planned activities aimed at addressing difficult and/or complex issues and opportunities that require an ongoing approach) and campaigns (shorter term, planned activities aimed at addressing a specific and time-limited issue or opportunity) effectively it is vitally important to look at the context in which public relations activity takes place, since this differs from organization to organization. It helps to look at the factors affecting organizations in a systematic way, and addressing the areas outlined in Figure 2.1 provides a blueprint for doing this.

This contextual research is not about specific public relations problems or opportunities necessarily (more of this in Chapter 3), but it is vital background information required in order to plan and manage effectively. As mentioned earlier, programmes and campaigns have to be seen with this wider context because issues and opportunities and the plans aimed at addressing them do not exist in isolation. These days everything is connected and the organization is looked at and judged as a whole, not as a set of discrete activities.

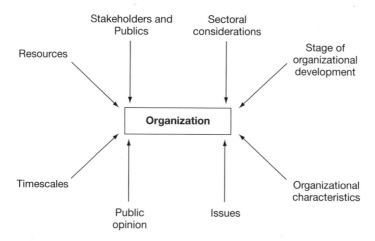

Figure 2.1 *Factors to be considered when researching the background for public relations activity*

STAKEHOLDERS AND PUBLICS

Chapter 6 has a much more detailed discussion on stakeholders and publics, but from the outset it is important that the public relations practitioner is aware of the whole range of stakeholders that must be communicated with. This will be a major factor in deciding the public relations task. Each stakeholder will have a different communication requirement, although the information given to each must not conflict.

Before going further, it is important to obtain clarity about terms. In public relations there are a group of terms that are often used interchangeably, but they have slightly different meanings.

The word 'stakeholder' rather than 'publics', is growing in popularity. The word was first brought to the fore by Freeman[1] in the debates on corporate governance in the United States in the 1980s. The view was that companies had a primary responsibility to shareholders, but Freeman insisted that there are others with a legitimate stake in the company. He defined stakeholders as 'those who are affected by, or who can affect' an organization.

For some organizations, their range of stakeholders can be quite small. For example, a niche manufacturer of mobile telephone parts will have a relatively contained group of stakeholders since they operate in a confined business-to-business environment and the end user of the telephone may not even know the company's name, or even that they exist: unless the part is faulty.

An organization such as the US Army, on the other hand, will have many stakeholders, not only in the United States, but also around the world. Indeed, it could be argued that ultimately just about everyone could have a stake in the US Army, because its presence is widespread and potentially it could be involved in operations in any part of the world. In addition, there are millions of people around the world who take a virtual stake in the US Army, discussing its activities online and sometimes using social networking sites and so on to organize virtual or physical protests, or to support action. However, to talk of everyone being a stakeholder is a difficult and imprac-tical notion to handle. Most organizations wish to identify those who they should prioritize because resources are limited. More on this in Chapter 6.

Publics are stakeholders, but they are stakeholders with a particular relationship with the organization. Grunig and Hunt[2] describe publics as those for whom an organization has created a problem or an issue. More commonly now, publics are described as stakeholders who become active either for or against the organization. The author's view is that publics combine both these factors: issues or opportunities, and activity.

Typically, stakeholders are categorized into broad groups that describe the nature of the stake. For example, shareholders, customers and employees are typical stakeholders. Publics on the other hand can be drawn from across all these groups and they coalesce around an issue. For example, a company may wish to close down a factory; this creates an issue for a range of stakeholders – employees, local shopkeepers, local community, suppliers, etc. They could all group together to oppose the closure: they are active and they are a recognizable and coherent group drawn together because of the issue.

Conversely, there are often important stakeholders who remain inactive. For example, there may be a number of individuals who have invested significant sums of money in a company. As long as there is a reasonable return on their investment they remain passive, even disinterested in the activities of the company. If, however, returns decline, they and other stakeholders may become active around this issue and therefore become a public.

The word 'audience' is sometimes used in public relations. Audiences are usually broad, undifferentiated groups, reflecting the fact that the word originates from the world of the mass media. Hence, TV and radio have audiences, and these not only comprise large numbers, but also include isolated individuals who are not organized into recognized groups.

Finally, 'target groups' is a term sometimes used in public relations. These are the groups at which the campaign or programme is aimed: it is their attitudes and behaviours that the originator of the communication wishes to affect in some way. They are not to be confused with intermediary individuals or groups who may receive communication (receivers), but then pass it on to the target group. So, for example, schoolteachers may be used to communicate information about summer holiday activities in the local park: the schoolteachers are the receivers of the information, but the school-children are the target group.

The object of the exercise in communication is to enlist the support of stakeholders and publics. Sometimes that support will need to be active and immediate, for example, an organization wanting customers to buy their products or voters to vote for your political party in tomorrow's general election. Sometimes the support is less active and not bound by specific timescales. For example, a company might organize a community relations campaign, simply because they feel it right to put something back into a community that provides most of its workforce. There might be no specific business objectives at the time of implementing the programme apart from to enhance the reputation of the company and build positive relationships generally. However, the feeling of goodwill that the campaign engenders may make recruitment easier or minimize the possibility of objections automatically being raised if they want to extend their factory in the future. Having undertaken a longer-term, goodwill-building programme they can, if they need to, switch more easily to a focused programme which seeks to enlist active support on particular issues.

With some publics a change in opinions and behaviour may be wanted, with others existing behaviour or opinions may need to be confirmed, and yet with others you might want to engender an opinion or pattern of behaviour may be wanted where previously that public was entirely neutral.

Factors to bear in mind when considering stakeholders and publics include the following:

- *Range.* That is the breadth of stakeholders and publics concerned. For some organizations, for example, a club for professional antique dealers, the range of publics may be very narrow. For other organizations, for instance, the Department of Health, the range of stakeholders and publics is very large indeed.
- *Numbers and location.* Some organizations have a range of stakeholders and publics that fall into large uniform blocks, for example, the multiple retailers will have large groups of customers, suppliers and local authorities as some of their stakeholders. Others, for example project engineers, will have a whole range of publics, often small in number, attached to each project. Some organizations have publics covering a wide geographical or socio-economic spread; others have very focused groups to concentrate on.
- *Influence and power.* Some publics, for example active pressure groups, can gain a great deal of power, particularly if they catch the public mood. They may not be large in number or have any direct link to the organization, but they can be highly influential over the way an organization conducts its business and are usually very skilled at putting together or linking with other networks with whom they can forge common ground,

especially online. Shell's reversal of its decision to sink the Brent Spar oil platform in the North Sea was forced by a relatively small, but highly effective organization (Greenpeace) galvanizing public opinion. In a different way, shareholders wield a great deal of power. They have an obvious stake in an organization and, although they can be few in number, can determine its future overnight. One of the tasks of the public relations practitioner is to determine the relative influence and power of all the publics concerned, and weight the public relations programme accordingly. This is not to say that the most powerful and influential publics always need to have the most attention, but obviously their concerns and communication needs are important.

- *Connection with organization.* Some publics are intimately connected with an organization, for example its employees. Others have a more remote connection, for example those making an occasional visit to the website. Some publics will have an amicable relationship with the organization, others will find themselves in opposition to it. Again, the public relations practitioner needs to have a clear perception of the nature of these relationships and to gauge their changing nature. Some relationships could be in danger of becoming distant or of deteriorating. Others may ameliorate over time and indeed turn from negative to positive, for example, if a pressure group's legitimate concerns are addressed. Some groups are always active, some very rarely. Furthermore, some publics may have very active sub-groups within them, whereas other sections of the same public may be apparently quiescent, but with the potential to become active. Shareholders and online communities are classic examples of this. Thus the needs not only of the whole group, but parts of it also need to be considered.

SECTORAL CONSIDERATIONS

The nature of the sector in which the organization operates will profoundly influence the way public relations is conducted. Public relations for a market-leading manufacturer of fast-moving consumer goods is quite different from public relations for a college of further education.

Each sector has its own particular opportunities, threats and constraints. Just some of the sectors in the public or non-profit-making area are:

- education;
- government departments;
- National Health Service (NHS), health and medical care;
- voluntary organizations;
- charities;
- emergency services;
- the armed services;

- NGOs (non-governmental organizations), for example the World Health Organization;
- local government.

Some of the organizations in these sectors are enormous and the public relations support required for a major government department such as the Department of Health or a large international charity such as Oxfam are as large or larger and as complex as anything that would be found in the private sector. In fact, because of the constraints placed on some of those organizations, for example the requirements of Freedom of Information legislation or the need to account for every single pound spent on promotional activity, the challenges can be seen to be greater than for those in private industry where it could be argued there is less direct external accountability.

The private sector, too, cannot be regarded as a uniform mass. It can be split up into the following areas:

- commerce;
- finance;
- manufacturing;
- services;
- retail.

The growing number of online businesses can almost be regarded as a sector in its own right.

Working in the manufacturing environment where there may be great emphasis on marketing communication activities that demonstrate a physical product, will require sales promotion contexts such as exhibitions, virtual and physical demonstrations, conferences, glossy brochures, etc, where the product can be touched and sampled, virtually or actually. This can be quite different from working in the service sector where the balance may be towards descriptive techniques such as case studies, testimonials, online advocacy sites and paper-based materials that give confidence in the people providing the service.

There is one other sector that does not fit neatly into either public or private and that is the professional service sector, such as accountancy, law and management consultancy.

ORGANIZATIONAL DEVELOPMENT – BUSINESS STAGE

Public relations activities are often dictated by the stage of development at which an organization finds itself.

Development depends on the sort of sector an organization operates within. For example, in the fashion or in the hi-tech industries, development and decline can be very rapid indeed. Other industries, the motor trade or food retailing being cases in point, mature more slowly and can maintain their position for many years. Ford Motor Company is a good example of a mature, established company, but even it was threatened in the economic crisis of 2009.

Then there are variations within industries. Apple's iphone grew rapidly in an industry dominated for many years by companies such as Nokia, Sony-Ericsson and Samsung.

Factors affecting organizational development are:

- the nature of the industry;
- competitor activity;
- technological impacts;
- the power of suppliers;
- the power of consumers;
- management decisions on direction;
- resources, both financial and human.

Looking at the various stages of an organization's development reveals that there will be specific public relations requirements at different times:

- *Start-up.* Usually companies start small. The owners may know suppliers, customers and their employees, and often there will not be a separate public relations function. Public relations will be in the form of one-to-one contact with the various publics, with maybe some literature and a website with various levels of interactivity to attract business and publicise the company. The main emphasis will be on marketing communication, since growth will be a priority.
- *Growth.* With more employees and more customers, face-to-face contact may not be possible and management time will be taken up managing the business. At this stage an individual public relations practitioner or a consultancy may be employed. Public relations may still be viewed quite narrowly, largely as part of the marketing communication mix. Externally activity will focus on raising awareness of the company, its products and services. Internally there may be the beginnings of a formal communication programme including briefings, use of online media, notice boards, social activities and so on.

  The priority will be on expansion, and capital costs could be quite high, especially if new premises have to be acquired. Resource constraints are likely to be a major factor influencing the role of public relations. Activities like a comprehensive community relations programme may be low on the agenda.

- *Maturity.* At this stage the organization is likely to be well established. The public relations function probably will be expanded and certainly the range of activities it is involved in is likely to be considerably broadened.

  It could well be that a stockmarket flotation is being considered. Capital might be needed for expansion or acquisition. If this is the case an active financial public relations campaign will be pursued.

  Employee relations will be more developed. The objective will be to have an efficient and well-motivated workforce who are working to agreed organizational objectives and who help to maintain a competitive edge. There will also be the need to attract good-quality new staff to the organization.

  Employee communications will be well developed, including techniques such as employee briefings, conferences, newsletters and the full range of online communication. Public relations may be involved in supporting other departments such as the training function in producing interactive training programmes, and HR in staff recruitment. Indeed, it will be advising a variety of managers and their departments on communication matters.

  The public relations department may be assisted by one or more public relations consultancies and will be running a full corporate programme as well as continuing to support marketing efforts. The organization should, at this stage, have a cohesive identity and an established reputation. Furthermore, it should have a developed sense of corporate responsibility, as it impacts more and more on the environment in which it operates (both local and remote). It will probably be involved actively in a range of community relations projects, including sponsorships, help in kind, support of local initiatives, cause-related marketing and so on.

  The public relations department will be using the full range of communication channels at its disposal and be interacting with a potentially large number of publics and stakeholders with a complex range of connections with both the organization and each other.

- *Decline.* Many companies avoid decline by adjusting their orientation or by moving into new areas of activity. However, for whatever reason, takeover, financial or legislative change, or downright bad management, some organizations move into a period of temporary or permanent decline. Even here there is a vital role for public relations to play. Spotting the issues before they become terminal crises is a key role (see Chapter 4 for more on this). Handling crises with honesty and integrity if they do happen (for example a major product recall, as in the case of Johnson & Johnson's handling of the Tylenol recall, or a major incident such as Richard Branson's handling of the Virgin train crash in Cumbria, UK in 2007, can help maintain reputation and minimize the risk of a crisis unravelling out of control.

29

Ultimately, if a business is non-viable, there is nothing public relations can do to rescue it. However, managing the expectations, and trying to influence the behaviour of those publics critical to the eventual fate of an organization in decline is very much within the remit of public relations. This is not a manipulative or unethical exercise, but it is managing the situation professionally, bearing in mind the legitimate interests of all those involved.

ORGANIZATIONAL CHARACTERISTICS

There should be no skeletons unknown to the public relations practitioner, who should know the organization inside out: history, its current status, its future plans, everything there is to know. The following headings give a framework for investigation:

- *Nature of sector.* Know the sector. What are the trends for the sector? Is it expanding, contracting and are there new, exciting markets? What is the operating environment? Is the economy in recession and are there any major issues facing the industry or the company, such as new legislation or pressing environmental demands? What is the reputation of the sector? If the sector as a whole has a bad reputation, this is an additional problem.
- *Competitor activity.* How is the organization placed in relation to the competition? Is it possible to take market leadership in some or all areas? Are competitors new, aggressive young Turks likely to steal the market? Are there few or many competitors? Which ones are making headway and why? What are their weaknesses? Are some smarter than others in using all communication channels and techniques effectively?
- *Mission.* What is the mission of the organization? Is it to be the biggest, the best, the most innovative? Is it possible to be distinctive or will it be a 'Me too'? Is the mission realistic or a pious hope which needs to be challenged? Will the mission be supported by stakeholders?
- *Size and structure.* How large is the organization compared to others inside and outside the sector? How much 'clout' does it have? Does it have a single, simple structure or is it a complex conglomerate? Is it hierarchical or flat, restructured or re-engineered? Does it operate in one or several countries? (Different countries have different reputations: an engineering company operating from Germany will be regarded differently from one operating from Ghana, where there is no established engineering tradition.) What is the structure of the public relations operation given these factors? Is it an appropriate structure? Should consultancies be used or should everything be handled in-house?

- *Nature of the organization.* What activities does the organization perform? Is it single or multi-product or service? Does it operate in a single sector or several sectors? Are specialist public relations skills and knowledge needed, for example is a lobbying division needed, or can all activities be served from a unified or devolved public relations department?
- *Tradition and history.* Is the company old and established or is it new with a position to establish? Is it well known for doing things in certain ways or is it an unknown quantity? Closely linked to this is the philosophy and culture of the organization. Is it open and participative or is it hierarchical and directive?
- *Image history.* How has the organization been perceived over the years? Is it market- or thought-leading, innovative, reliable, plodding and slow, or slightly shifty? Has the image been constant or has it been subject to rapid or developmental change?
- *Types of employees.* White collar? Blue collar? Graduate? Semi- or unskilled? A complete mixture?

All these organizational factors profoundly affect how the public relations function is structured, and how and what the activities are that need to be carried out.

ISSUES

It is obvious that the issues affecting the society or an industry in which an organization operates, as well as the specific issues that the organization faces, are likely to set an agenda for much of the public relations work. Issues generally fall into a number of categories, as follows:

- *Structural.* The major long-term trends in society, such as an ageing population, globalization, technological developments: things over which the individual organization will have very little control, but of which it needs to be aware.
- *External.* Largely contextual issues such as environmental concerns, community concerns, political imperatives.
- *Crises.* Normally short term and arising from unforeseen events, for example a factory disaster, war, product recall. However, sometimes crises have long-term effects on the organization's reputation. Arthur Andersen, the accounting firm, went out of business because of its links to the Enron scandal.
- *Internal.* Long- or short-term issues that the company faces from within, for example succession policy, industrial relations and organizational change.

- *Current affairs.* Those things that are of immediate public interest and which often are the subject of intense media coverage at the time, for example, dangerous dogs legislation following a series of dog attacks reported in the media, gun and knife legislation.
- *Potential.* Those issues that have not yet emerged. It might seem rather odd to list this, but it is very much the case that some issues do appear to arise from nowhere, except that the careful practitioner will have an intelligence system at his or her disposal that can give early warning of potential issues likely to become real. Content analysis of the media and of online sources can often give an indicator of what may be on the public agenda in the future, and is a vastly underutilized resource by organizations. Also, contact with think tanks, the scientific community and futures groups can provide a rich picture of possible scenarios.

The identification and handling of issues is a core skill of senior public relations practitioners, and a prized contribution that can be made to the organization. As the 2007 Arthur W Page Society Report, The Authentic Enterprise[3], points out, senior managers value someone with the equivalent of a crystal ball, who can tell them the issues they face, before they hit the organization. This is a key function of risk management and it is not an accident that some Board-level practitioners are dubbed the Chief Risk Manager – risks to reputation and in relationships that is.

This area of public relations work is of increasing importance, especially since online communities can collect around an issue very quickly and pose a threat to the organization. As one CEO has said, 'I used to be threatened by a city analyst and I had many days notice of impending problems. I am now threatened by a spotty youth using a computer in their bedroom, and I have no notice of either the issue or the time of attack.'[4] Hence, careful monitoring of online chatter and a connection to popular sites and services is vital. If only a few hours' notice is given for a significant issue, that is valuable time to engage with a response which deflates the issue, or buy some time for a more studied response to prepare for a crisis, or alert others who may act as sources of authoritative information or act as advocates.

PUBLIC OPINION

Public opinion, often expressed through or led by the traditional media or, increasingly, online sources, is a very potent influence on organizations. The campaign against genetically modified organisms in the United Kingdom led to the withdrawal of genetically modified foods from many supermarkets. Those at the forefront of research in this area, for example Monsanto, had to modify their plans for development as a result and government-approved trials were disrupted.

The on- and offline media as reflectors of public opinion are vital to public relations because the same channels are often used by public relations as a means of information and engagement. The media often define and crystallize the public mood, although sometimes its influence can be overestimated.

It is certainly true that these media can fatally damage the reputation of an organization or individual. Sometimes this is because the organization is genuinely at fault, in which case the media is doing its job of serving the public interest. Sometimes, as libel cases attest, there is little ground for their attacks.

It is also the case that the media can massively enhance the reputation of an organization by, for example, endorsing its products or by favourably reporting on its performance. This is especially true if comment is made in influential media such as the *Financial Times* if a financial matter is being reported, or in the tabloids, consumer press and online magazines if a consumer product is being promoted.

TIMESCALES

Obviously timescales are critical when determining public relations programmes; this topic is discussed in detail in Chapter 8, but covered briefly here. Sometimes the practitioner has the luxury of planning a programme over a self-determined period of time. The research done by Gregory and Edwards in 2004[5] with the UK's Most Admired Companies indicated that up to 70 per cent of activity was planned. However, external or internal restraints, or both, can determine when activities can be performed.

- *Externally driven timescales.* External factors that might impact on how activities are planned include parliamentary timetables: if an organization wants to change a clause in some proposed legislation, it has to undertake its lobbying within the time frame laid down by Parliament. Financial results are regulated by the Stock Exchange rules. These are known external factors, but sometimes programmes have to be altered because of unknown factors which then require a reaction. For example, information regarding competitive activity may lead to pre-emptive action within very precise time limits. A breaking news story may provide an unexpected opportunity to action the programme earlier to good effect.
- *Internally driven timescales.* Examples of internally imposed deadlines are the introduction of a new product or service, a decision to build a new production line, achievement of an international quality standard, staff awards and so on.

RESOURCES

The level of resources put into a public relations function or department clearly determines the level and scope of activities that can be undertaken. The resourcing of specific programmes is discussed in Chapter 8. However, it is appropriate here to cover it briefly.

Normally there are two approaches. The first is to determine an appropriate departmental structure along with the relevant activities that need to be undertaken, and to provide the human and financial resources to implement them.

The second approach is to devote a budget to public relations determined by some internal resource allocation model. The trick then is to prioritize the public relations activities and to carry out those essential elements of the programme within budget.

While the first six areas give an overall context to public relations, it is true to say that timescales and resources are controlling factors on activity.

Notes

1. Freeman, R E (1984) *Strategic Management; a stakeholder approach*, Pitman, Boston, MA.
2. Grunig, J E and Hunt, T (1984) *Managing Public Relations*, Holt, Rinehart and Winston, New York.
3. Available at www.arthurwpagesociety.org.
4. Conversation reported to the author.
5. Gregory, A and Edwards, L (2004) Patterns of PR in Britain's Most Admired Companies. Report commissioned by Eloqui Pubic Relations from The Centre for Public Relations Studies, Leeds Business School, Leeds Metropolitan University.

3

Starting the planning process

RESPONSIBILITIES OF PRACTITIONERS

Having looked at public relations within the organizational context and recognizing the ways in which public relations can make a contribution to the organization and how it can be structured and conducted, we can now look at planning programmes in detail.

Public relations practitioners as members of their organizations have two sets of responsibilities. First of all they have organizational responsibilities like anyone else who works in a disciplined environment. They are public relations specialists and are responsible for discharging their specialized work to the best of their abilities. In addition to this, if they hold a management or supervisory role they have to handle budgets and people, run an effective department or consultancy, control suppliers, ensure quality standards are met and so on. In fact, all the skills required of any manager are required of public relations professionals.

There are also a number of other pressures. Much of the work is high profile. A mistake made when working with a journalist or influential blogger has very public consequences. In fact, most of the activities of public relations professionals are by definition 'public'. It's a profession where there are very few ground rules: the practice is not highly prescribed as it is for other professions, such as accountancy and law. The work is usually driven by deadlines and demand. When dealing with an issue or crisis it is impossible to predict how large 'the job' will be. There are severe qualitative and quantitative pressures on practitioners.

The public relations brief is a large and complex one: to manage the relationship and reputational interface between the organization and all its publics, either as a department or with others.

Hence, a systematic, efficient approach is essential. As far as possible there has to be a measure of control, although total control in the dynamic world of public relations is impossible and not even desirable.

PUBLIC RELATIONS POLICY

Given that public relations practitioners are not solely responsible for building relationships with stakeholders and publics, the first requirement is for a clear public relations policy to be laid down. This should define the remit of public relations activity and set the ground rules for operation.

The idea of a policy is not to be regulatory and restrictive, but to give the rules of engagement so that everyone knows where responsibility lies, where the lines of demarcation are and, ultimately, who is accountable for what activities.

Policy statements need not be long or complicated, but they must be clear.

Figure 3.1 shows an example from Pilkington PLC of its corporate public relations policy. Pilkington has a group (corporate) public relations function which deals largely with company-wide matters and which agreed this policy with senior management. It also has several divisions and subsidiaries that have their own public relations activities.

CORPORATE PUBLIC RELATIONS POLICY

1. Meetings with the City press must be kept at a level consistent with maintaining satisfactory relationships and will be arranged through Group Public Relations.

   Statements to the City press may be made only by General Board directors, or by Group Public Relations acting on the Board's instructions.

2. The Group will not normally publicize through the media its attitudes to matters that are politically sensitive at local or national level. Considerable time is expended by directors and some senior managers on representing the

---

company's interests to legislators, parliamentarians, and others with the ability to affect the company's future; these contacts can be prejudiced by inopportune publicity.

3. The Group will not offer public comment on the wisdom or otherwise of budgetary or other legislative measures. It may be prepared to give factual evidence about the effects of such measures on the performance of any part of the Group when such effects can be demonstrated.

4. Public comment, in the press or elsewhere, must relate to historic or current activities. Comment about future plans and/or prospects must be avoided so far as is practicable.

5. Announcements about possible or planned capital investments or disinvestments may not normally be made until such projects have been formally authorized by the General Board.

   Where local or national government agencies need to be consulted in advance of an investment, it may be necessary to make an earlier announcement. In such cases, the limited extent of the commitment at that stage must be emphasized. Dates for starting or completing projects must be given in a form that will allow for contingencies.

6. No announcements should be made about negotiations, eg licensing agreements, co-operative agreements with other companies, until negotiations are successfully completed and the form of announcement has been agreed by the parties concerned.

7. Opportunities for favourable publicity will be identified by Group Public Relations and exploited after clearance at Executive Director level.

8. Divisions, subsidiaries and functions retaining external public relations advisers in whatever capacity should ensure that the constraints of their role are very clearly defined, if necessary in consultation with Group Public Relations.

   Under no circumstances must retained advisers be permitted to make public statements on behalf of Pilkington, or to lobby on behalf of Pilkington, without prior clearance through Group Public Relations.

9. Where circumstances suggest that action should be taken which would be at variance with these guidelines, such action should not be taken without prior clearance from the Chairman or a Deputy Chairman, with the involvement of Group Public Relations.

10. Divisions, subsidiaries and functions should ensure that Group Public Relations are briefed and consulted on all occasions where these guidelines have a relevance.

    These guidelines are not intended to restrict divisional public relations activities in the marketing area where there is established liaison with Group Public Relations.

Figure 3.1 *Pilkington PLC corporate public relations policy*

Once public relations policy has been confirmed, activities can be planned and managed appropriately.

WHY PLANNING IS IMPORTANT

It is quite legitimate to ask 'Why plan?' There is always so much to do, why not just get on and do it?

Apart from the vital fact of putting some order into working life, as discussed in Chapter 1, there are several other good reasons for planning:

- *It focuses effort.* It ensures the unnecessary is excluded. It makes practitioners work on the right things. It helps them to work smart instead of just working hard. It enables them to operate efficiently and effectively because they are concentrating on the things that have been deemed important.
- *It improves effectiveness.* By working on the right things, defined objectives will be achieved. Time and money will be saved because effort isn't being diverted into worthy but less important tasks. Importantly it makes saying 'No' to unplanned things much easier. Or at least there can be discussion along the lines of, 'If I take on this task, which of my other prioritized jobs should I drop?' or, 'If this task is necesary, we need to employ extra support'. In other words, working to planned objectives gives targets to aim for, a sense of achievement when they are reached, and effective benchmarks for measurement.
- *It encourages the long-term view.* By definition, to plan requires looking forward. This forces a longer perspective than the immediate here and now. It requires a look back to evaluate past achievements, a look around at the organization and its priorities and at the broader organizational context, and it helps produce a structured programme to meet future as well as current needs.
- *It helps demonstrate value for money.* If there is a fight for budgets or a need to project a return on investment, then demonstrating past achievements and being able to present a powerful, costed, forward-looking and realistic programme gives a point from which to argue a case for money.
- *It minimizes mishaps.* Careful planning means that different scenarios will have been considered and the most appropriate selected. It means that there will be meticulous contingency planning and all the angles will have been covered. As far as possible all the potential problems and issues will have been identified and addressed.
- *It reconciles conflicts.* When putting together a programme or a campaign there are always conflicts of interests and priorities. Planning helps practitioners confront those difficulties before they arise and to work them through to resolution. Sometimes this can mean difficult discussions with and decisions about other colleagues in different departments, but better to sort that out at the planning stage than in the middle of a complex, time-constrained programme. Furthermore, if

external stakeholders and publics are involved in planning campaigns, their potential issues and conflicts can be addressed at an early stage.

● *It facilitates proactivity.* Practitioners setting their own agenda is vitally important. Of course public relations work is about reacting to media demands or responding quickly to a crisis, but it is also about deciding what is important – what actions should be taken, and when. Planning a comprehensive and cohesive programme helps achieve this.

Planning applies to everything, whether it is to complete campaigns and programmes lasting one or several years or even longer, or to individual activities such as an event or a new publication.

BASIC QUESTIONS IN PLANNING

The planning process has a number of logical steps that break down into a manageable sequence. It is helpful to ask five basic questions:

What do I want to achieve?	(What are my objectives?)
Who do I want to talk to?	(Who are my stakeholders and publics?)
What do I want to say?	(What is the content I want to get across or the dialogue I want to initiate?)
How shall I say it?	(What mechanisms shall I use to get my content or dialogue across?)
How do I know I've got it right?	(How will I evaluate my work?)

The purpose of the activity is to influence attitudes, opinions or behaviour in some way. It is also to listen to stakeholders and publics to see whether the organization needs to change in order to maintain support and approval.

In order to answer the questions posed above there are two major requirements:

● *Information.* Finding out everything there is to know about the task in hand – careful research and analysis.
● *Strategy.* Using that information to identify the guiding principles and main thrust of the programme.

From these two requirements comes the tactical programme that can be evaluated for effectiveness.

At this stage it should be noted that the list of questions includes questions about information-seeking and research (objectives, publics, messages and evaluation), but only one question about the actual doing.

This is about the right proportion of effort that should go into the planning process. Get the research and analysis right, and the programme should then virtually write itself. Please note, it is not being suggested that 80 per cent of the time spent on a programme overall should be put into information-seeking. That is plainly wrong as nothing would be achieved on time. However, 80 per cent of the effort put into devising an appropriate programme should go into the first stages. Once having put all that work into planning, the implementation has a much greater likelihood of running smoothly and effectively.

All planning models follow a similar pattern, whether they are for the strategic management of an organization or for a public relations programme. There are four basic steps as shown in Figure 3.2.

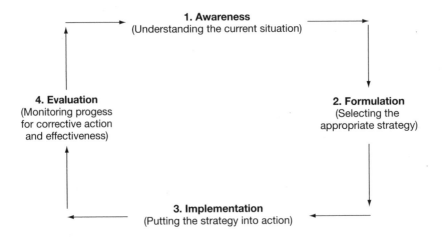

Figure 3.2 *The strategic management process*

US academics Scott Cutlip, Allen Center and Glen Broom[1] visualize the planning and management of public relations programmes as shown in Figure 3.3.

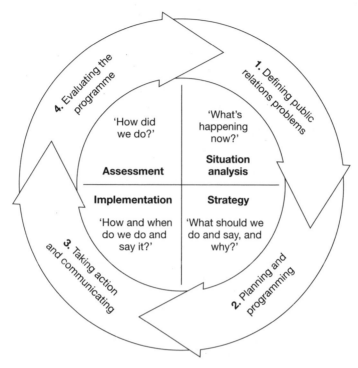

Figure 3.3 *Cutlip, Center and Broom's planning and management model*

THE 12 STAGES OF PLANNING

To expand on the above, we can look at a sequence of planning steps that will ensure an effective programme (an ongoing employee relations programme or individual campaign) is put together:

- analysis;
- aims;
- objectives;
- stakeholders and publics;
- content;
- strategy;
- tactics;
- timescales;
- resources;
- monitoring;
- evaluation;
- review.

The planning process is illustrated in Figure 3.4.

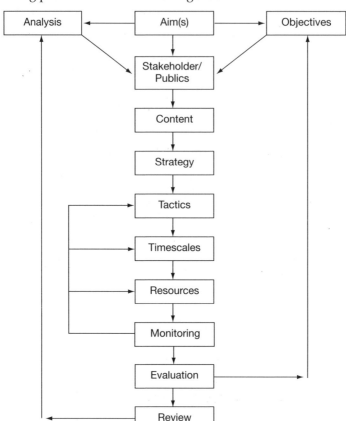

Figure 3.4 *The planning process in logical steps*

Sometimes the analysis and objectives are in reverse order. An organization might give its public relations department or consultancy a list of objectives it wants them to achieve. However, these objectives must be carefully scrutinized in order to see if they are appropriate and to ensure the objective is a public relations objective or whether it masks a problem that cannot be solved by public relations alone. For example, the organization may say it has a problem recruiting good new staff, in which case the public relations objective would be to help attract new recruits from the community and could commission a communication campaign designed to do just that. However, after careful analysis, the public relations professionals may discover that the real problem is not recruitment, but retention of good staff, thus the objectives of the programme will have to change and an internal rather than external campaign will have to be mounted which addresses employment policies and perhaps cultural issues within the workplace. These problems will require more than communications to solve them.

The planning process looks quite straightforward when laid out as it is in Figure 3.4. However, there are often problems in practice. Sometimes there is a lack of detailed information on which to base the plan. This may be because senior managers are sometimes reluctant to share all the context or details of the situation, or it may be that a client only wants to give a consultancy limited information for reasons of confidentiality. Perhaps the campaign itself is very complex or fast moving, for example a complicated takeover bid. It could be that the plan is being executed under extreme time pressure, in a crisis even. It is often the case that the resources devoted to programmes are less than ideal and so corners have to be cut or the programme pruned. There also is the possibility that there are other issues that emerge part-way through the programme that require energy and resources to be diverted from the original course of action.

However, the planning scheme outlined gives a solid basis for planning and the template can be followed whatever the scale of the task. If the programme is particularly large it may be necessary to split it down into a series of smaller projects that follow the same steps. Thus there might be a public affairs programme and a community relations programme, each with focused objectives and different publics, which feed into an overall programme with wider objectives and broader stakeholders, publics and messages. This is illustrated in Figure 3.5.

There are two things that should be noted. First, objectives need to be tied into organizational objectives (see Chapter 5). Second, as described here, the planning process could be perceived to be mechanistic and inflexible. This is not the case. The process described gives a framework for planning. In reality, time and events move on, sometimes very quickly, and public relations practitioners must be prepared to respond to changing circumstances. All the best-laid plans must be capable of being flexed or developed, and indeed scrapped altogether if necessary. Furthermore, it can well be that if an activity has become somewhat routinized, for example an AGM that has a specific format that is adhered to year on year, then the planning template can be used more as a mental checklist to ensure that all the usual areas are covered and to ask sensible questions about whether certain elements have changed or need refreshing. When working with other colleagues, having a framework that conforms to recognized planning disciplines does provide structure and coherence. The absence of a plan can otherwise indicate the lack of a strategic approach and sometimes a lack of capability. A plan indicates professionalism and accountability. It is an indicator of good management and not only assures the organization that public relations will make a valuable and agreed contribution, but provides security and a level of stability for the practitioner.

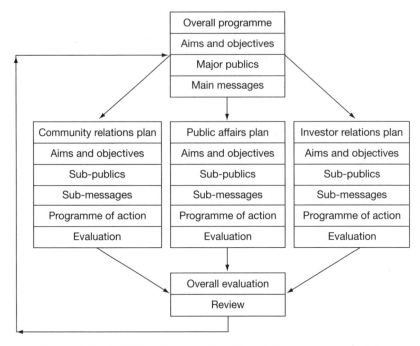

Figure 3.5 *Splitting the overall public relations programme into
manageable sub-sections*

It is important to stress that planning is an aid to effective working and not
an end in itself. It is not meant to be a straitjacket; neither does it guarantee
success. A good plan in and of itself will not make unimaginative or poorly
executed programmes work. In addition, as suggested earlier, flexibility
and adaptability are essential. In public relations, of all disciplines, there
has to be a capability to react and adjust to the dynamic organizational and
communication environment in which we operate. Sometimes objectives
and tactics have to change – rapidly. That is a factor of organizational life.

Plans are made to ensure that priorities are focused on and achieved. The
planning process holds good, even if programmes themselves have to be
adjusted. The steps given in Figure 3.2 can be followed whatever changes
are needed.

LINKING PROGRAMME PLANNING TO THE BIGGER PICTURE

To illustrate the links between the planning sequence described in this
chapter within the wider organizational context discussed in Chapters 1
and 2, Figure 3.6 provides an example.

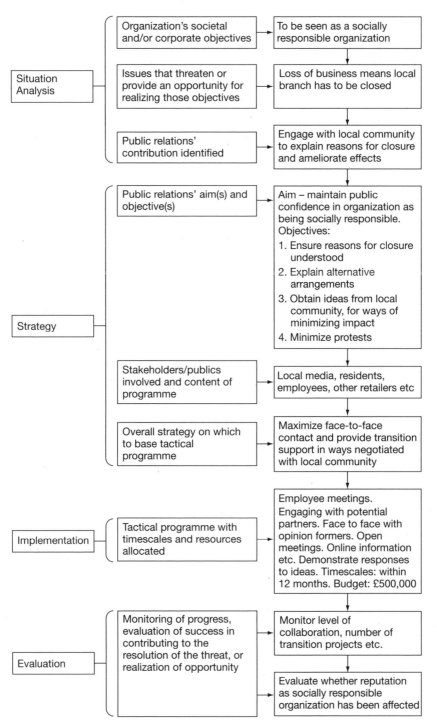

Figure 3.6 *A comprehensive planning model*

Note

1. Cutlip, S M, Center, A H and Broom, G N (2006) *Effective Public Relations*, Prentice-Hall International, Upper Saddle River, NJ, 9th edn.

4

Research and analysis

Before going into more detail about the elements of the planning process outlined in Chapter 5, it is vital to stress the importance of research. A hallmark of strategic public relations programmes is that they are founded on research and that research permeates the whole process.

EMBEDDING RESEARCH IN THE PLANNING PROCESS

In recent years there has been a drive in both the public and private sectors, to have evidence-based inputs to decision making. It is true that some insightful entrepreneurs have 'hunches' that work, but even here, the evidence is that they are finely attuned to what their stakeholders' aspirations are, and that comes by being deeply informed about the stakeholders themselves and what is going on in the wider world that is affecting stakeholder attitudes and behaviours. Most people do not have that intuition, and even if they have, intuition should be tested to determine whether it is based in reality.

Again, within organizations, those proposing plans are expected to present a 'business case', or a compelling argument for why their plans should be accepted. For public relations this will not just be about resources, but there will be an evidence-based case for why particular issues should be addressed, which relationships should be invested in, and what the require-ments are if the organization's reputation is to be protected, maintained or enhanced. Furthermore, once the plan is implemented, it will be expected that the promised 'returns' can be evidenced as being realized. Public rela-tions plans should therefore follow these expected disciplines. Indeed, research should be seen to inform all stages of the plan if it is to stand up to scrutiny. Combining the four major stages of planning suggested by Cutlip, Centre and Broom in Figure 3.3, with the 12-step planning template given in Figure 3.4, provides a model for describing the type of research needed for any plan, as Figure 4.1 demonstrates.

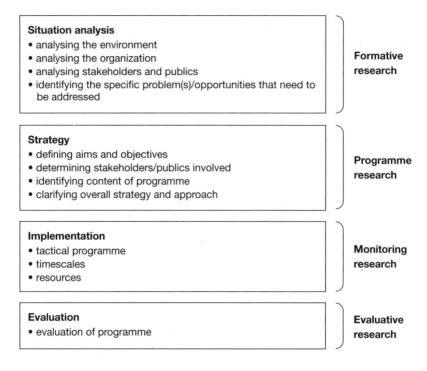

Figure 4.1 *Embedding research in the planning process*

Formative research is undertaken to gather and interpret the data (intelli-gence) that helps you to identify the real issues, problems and opportuni-ties within a specific time and events context. A proper understanding of the situation is the essential foundation of any strategic plan. Key questions at this stage are 'what', 'why' and 'who'. What is going on, why and with whom?

Programme research aims at ensuring that the proposed plan of action is properly thought-through and informed. Key questions here are 'who', 'how' and 'what'. Who is it we need to engage with? How will we engage with them? What are our objectives and how will we measure success at the end of the programme? How are they likely to respond? What are the intended and unintended consequences of our engagement? This will involve, for example, pre-testing of ideas, research on the suitability of the channels of communication to be used, pilot testing of content, pilot testing of reactions to the proposed programme: all research-based activities.

Monitoring research is designed to check whether the programme is on-track as it is being implemented. Key questions here are 'what' and 'how'. How is the programme developing and what are the responses? How do we need to adjust the programme? Questions should also be asked about programme management: are the timescales likely to be achieved? Are resources adequate or too much? Can we make management of the programme more effective and efficient by cutting out what appear to be redundant activities? What will the impact of that be?

Evaluative research determines whether the programme achieved its declared objectives, or outcomes. Key questions are 'what' and 'why'. What did we achieve? Were our objectives realistic? If not, how should we have framed them, or were there other factors to take into account? What did we do well? What did we not do well and why? What lessons can we learn? What can we build on for the future? What were the unintended effects and why did we not identify these? What have we contributed to the organization as a result of this programme? A hard look at the evaluation techniques used also needs to be undertaken at this stage. Did they produce the information required for correct judgements about the success of the programme to be made, or would other types of evaluation have been more appropriate? Were there other unexpected outcomes that also need to be evaluated, and if so, how? For example, it may be that a consultancy was aiming a recycling campaign at people taking packed lunches to work, but an unintended and good effect is that their children also became enthusiastic about recycling, and contributed significantly to the results of the campaign.

A case study showing how research was embedded in the 2012 Olympic bid programme for London is given in Chapter 9.

Having outlined the role of research in the whole of the planning process, it is now appropriate to focus on the formative research element: situation analysis.

THE FIRST PLANNING STEP

Analysis is the first part of the planning process. This entails research in order to identify the context and issues on which to base public relations programmes. Without getting to the core issues there will not be a credible or effective programme, or one that supports organizational objectives.

If a core issue is that the organization and products are regarded as old-fashioned and therefore it is losing credibility and market share, the programme will have to be about demonstrating that the organization is forward looking and their products are modern and leading edge (provided that they are), not that theirs are cheaper than their competitors.

There isn't room in this book to look at the whole area of research in public relations. Complete volumes have been written on the subject. However, it is possible to give an overview.

When starting a department or a full programme from scratch (for example, following a large merger), the contextual research outlined in Chapter 2 is vital. However, if the public relations function is established and the planned programme or campaign is a continuation of an ongoing activity, then a judgement will have to be made about how much of the full analysis should be made. Nevertheless, a mental check-through of the process is necesary, even if it is just a case of confirming that a full exploration of all the steps is not necessary. It should be borne in mind, however, that it is important and illuminating to conduct this contextual research from time to time and some of it (for example, media content monitoring and checking stakeholder perceptions) should be ongoing anyway.

As indicated at the beginning of this chapter, for new campaigns or programmes it is vitally important to undertake a situation analysis – formative research. This research falls under four headings: a) analysing the environment; b) the organization; c) stakeholders and publics; and d) identifying and clarifying the specific issues (positive and/or negative) that need to be addressed.

If a new department is being established or all public relations activities are being reviewed, this sequence will be the one to follow to establish a series of programmes and campaigns. Sometimes, however, an issue is apparent or the practitioner is presented with an issue to solve. Here it is important to undertake some initial clarification of the issue, while using the first three steps to provide context, deeper understanding and a measure of the task in hand. For example, suppose a charity is experiencing a decline in the number of volunteers and public relations is asked to mount a campaign to reverse the trend. The analysis sequence and questions might be something like this:

Initial clarification:

- How long have numbers been declining?
- What are the demographics of our volunteers (eg age, gender, geography, income)? Can we draw conclusions about which groups in the volunteer community are declining?
- What are the travel patterns of our volunteers?
- What type of work is most/least popular, etc?

Analysis of the environment:

- What are the broader social changes that might affect volunteering?
- Are there pertinent economic changes?
- Are there regulatory constraints? For example, new legislation affecting those who interact with vulnerable adults? And so on.

Analysis of the organization:

- Have there been changes in the organization that might affect volunteers, eg the way we communicate, travel expenses policy, management changes, changes in the location of premises, working hours, etc.

Stakeholders and publics:

- Who is involved? Do we have a deep understanding of our volunteers and of their issues and aspirations? Why do they volunteer? Why do they think numbers are declining?
- Who else is involved? How? Why? What is the nature of their stake?
- Who else should be involved? How? Why? etc.

Having given a brief example, therefore, of the analysis that might be undertaken by this charity, it is appropriate to take a more detailed look at each of these steps in turn.

ANALYSING THE ENVIRONMENT

The analysis of both external and internal context is called 'environmental monitoring' in the public relations literature. It is important because wider issues in the environment often require organizations to act or react and action always has a communication dimension. Furthermore, the changing external environment, usually outside the ability of any one organization to control, often affects employees in their other lives and shapes the future. For example, the impact of globalization now has to be factored into the way organizations make their decisions and those who ignore this imperative will find themselves in difficulties.

Thus, the external environment might be described as containing the 'big picture' issues that set the organizational context. They arise from the actions of governments, and other regulatory organizations, from economic and social trends and from developments in science and technology. The macro environment is external to the organization and it is important to know about the external forces that are impacting on both the organization itself and its internal and external publics. The pressures, issues and imperatives that provide the context for the attitudes and decisions of publics need to be known by the public relations practitioner so that he or she can frame a programme with these matters taken into account. The external environment is of course both a very large and a very complex concept. Thus, to help frame thinking in this area, tools from the business literature can be borrowed.

PEST analysis

A commonly used and immensely valuable technique for analysing the external environment is PEST analysis. PEST divides the overall environment into four categories and covers most things that can affect an organization. The four areas are: **P**olitical, **E**conomic, **S**ocial and **T**echnological.

The main questions to ask when undertaking a PEST analysis are:

- What are the environmental factors that affect the organization?
- Which of these are currently most important?
- Which will be most important in the next four years?

For public relations practitioners other questions need to be asked:

- How will these factors impact on our reputation?
- How will they impact on our existing relationships? Will we need to develop new ones? With whom?
- Will these factors mean we have to change the culture of our organization?

The grid on the next page gives some headings that could be considered under the four areas.

POLITICAL	ECONOMIC
Environmental legislation	Interest rates
Employment legislation	Inflation
Trade (including overseas) legislation	Money supply
Change/continuance of government	Levels of empoyment
Political alliances within and between countries	Disposable income
	Business/economic cycles
	World business/economic conditions
	Energy costs
SOCIAL	TECHNOLOGICAL
Population shifts and growth	New discoveries
Lifestyles	Rate of change
Levels of education	Investment in technology
Income/wealth distribution	Spending on research and deveopment
Consumer purchasing trends	Obsolescence
Social attitudes and concerns	Impact of and access to new technologies
Purchasing habits	

Some experts recommend an expanded version of PEST, believing the original no longer does justice to the complex environment in which modern organizations operate. A popular acronym is EPISTLE. Here, as well as the four elements of PEST, separate consideration is given to Information, the Legal (or regulatory) aspects and the physical (or Green) Environment. Information, as they say, is power. Thus the access to and availability of information is critical to organizations. The ubiquity and power of the internet and its ability to empower stakeholders and publics makes this element of the environment even more potent. Conversely, it also means that those without the skills of access to technology will become increasingly disenfranchized. It also makes the communication challenge with these people and groups even more important to remember.

The legal environment in which organizations operate is increasingly complex and apart from national considerations there are transnational regulations such as EU law and international agreements such as those made by G20 and G8 members. Furthermore, there are quasi-legal restraints, including the 'moral' undertakings that governments make, such as the commitment to reduce greenhouse gases, in which organizations have a part to play.

The physical environment in which we live is judged to be one of *the* major concerns of the 21st century. The impact of global warming, pressures to radically alter transport systems, sustainability, waste disposal, etc, are all 'hot' topics and organizations will need to be aware of the drivers for change and the issues facing them as a result.

In addition, some analysts recommend that 'culture' merits specific consideration. Organizations need to recognize and take into account the diverse religious, ethnic and social cultures prevalent in the different countries in which they operate or trade. Also, sensitivity is required to organizational culture that reflect these differences and the different norms and values that mark out the 'distinctiveness' between organizations that work even within the same sector. Virgin is very different from Singapore Airlines.

The point of doing such analyses is to identify the main drivers that will impact on the organization. These drivers will be different, depending on the country, industry and organization being analysed – there are no stock responses.

It is also important to establish the interrelationships between these drivers. World economic trends may affect political decisions and technological developments may affect social aspects of life. For example, the technological developments in games technology has transformed the lives of many young people, especially boys, and has social consequences that have prompted political action. Gaming has also opened up opportunities in education and training and the sophisticated simulations generated by the industry have spilled over into military simulations.

Having generated a list of possible external environmental influences, the most relevant ones have to be identified, and it is imperative to be as specific as possible to the organization under consideration. So, for example, someone working in the higher education field in the Western world will have to consider the following three drivers among others. The first is to do with demographics; the proportion of people under 21 is decreasing so the higher education system will have to compete more fiercely for this 'traditional' source of students. The second is that the use of technology in teaching is transforming the traditional teacher/student relationship. Teachers are becoming facilitators of learning, helping students to navigate a whole range of alternative sources of information. Third, the requirement for the population to constantly update their knowledge and be retrained for different careers means there will be more mature students in the higher education system requiring a different educational experience from 'traditional' learners. This will demand greater flexibility and a wider range of skills of teaching staff, and the funding of these students will be on a different basis.

The PEST analysis process can also identify how external influences can affect organizations in different ways. So a company that traditionally sources its raw materials from a number of countries is less likely to be vulnerable to a political crisis than a company that sources its raw materials from a single, cheaper supplier in a country with a less stable political regime.

Some organizations are more affected by one of the four PEST areas than others. For example, the political context is vitally important to local government, whereas economic factors may be more important to retailing organizations.

Some of the 'big picture' issues facing most organizations and with profound communication ramifications are: globalization; the impact of technology (especially the internet); a culture of consumerism and consumer attitudes; diversity; individualism; the fragmentation of the media; mass migration and demographic changes.

Issues management

PEST analyses are done at particular points in time – something that is sometimes forgotten. They should be undertaken for the current situation and for different situations that might occur in the future. So in scenario planning, the most likely key drivers are given different weightings and alternative futures are envisaged, together with associated plans of action.

By carrying out a thorough-going PEST analysis, which looks not only at current but also future developments, it is possible to identify the potentially most significant issues that might affect the organization and to track those issues. A number of organizations such as universities and Think Tanks, eg The Work Foundation, DEMOS, Royal Society of Arts, and research companies such as IPSOS MORI, undertake regular futures research. In addition, the media monitoring companies now offer an issues analysis service. They not only track what are the most prevalent issues of the day overall (for example, views on current economic performance), but also spot those issues that are emerging on to the agenda because they are beginning to attract on- and offline comment and media coverage.

Forward-loooking companies spend a great deal of time and effort on issues management. They constantly scan the wider environment to determine which issues they should be paying particular regard to. Issues that are not identified or not taken seriously have a nasty habit of coming back as crises.

Issues management works in two ways:

● It identifies those issues over which the organization can have no control, where public opinion is inevitably going to move in a particular direction and therefore it would be foolish for the company to maintain or take up a position that flies in the face of the prevailing view. It would be very odd if an organization in the West were to promulgate the view that large families are to be encouraged when a major concern is overpopulation.

In this situation an organization has to examine its policies and practices, and bring them into line with public opinion, or it risks losing the sympathy and support of its stakeholders.

Organizations that are adept at issues management not only handle current issues, but also predict the likely public reaction to emerging concerns and position themselves as leaders by changing their policies and practices or adopting new ones ahead of anyone else. They can be seen to be leading the field rather than being forced to react because of prevailing opinion. They do this not just to get ahead, but because they are progressive, ethical, responsive to the likely demands of their stakeholders and sensitive to the wider responsibility they have to society.

- It detects those issues where the organization can have an input into the emerging debate and therefore shape its outcome in an ethical and beneficial way. An example of this was Rhone-Poulenc Agriculture's 10-year experiment looking at organic versus conventional farming (ie farming with agro-chemicals), which provided scientific evidence to determine the best farming method, economically, environmentally and in food quality terms. By establishing the facts about both systems, the company was able to make a definitive contribution to the debate.

Thus issues analysis works in both directions: detecting those external factors, political, economic, social or technological that require the company to change; and identifying those areas where it might have an input into the public debate and influence the outcome.

Company   Exchange and Effect   Issue

Any comprehensive public relations programme must address long-term issues. Individual public relations campaigns must also identify any relevant issues which, depending on the nature of the campaign, may be long or short term. Obviously a campaign to launch an individual car care product will not require such a wide-ranging examination of the issues as a five-year programme to relaunch and reposition a charity.

A note of caution on undertaking research on the external environment. This is a difficult and complex job and can be too large for a single individual or public relations department to undertake alone. Working with other colleagues in the organization, or employing skilled external consultants to help, both with the collection of information and its interpretation, can be a wise investment. The case study on the companion website for the book shows how Echo Research is tracking media issues for EADS and how this contributes to EADS' overall public relations intelligence-gathering activities. Please go to www.koganpage.com/PlanningAndManagingPublic RelationsCampaigns, where you will find the EADS case study.

In summary, it is important to know the broad organizational context, the issues affecting the organization now and into the future and to make informed decisions about how the organization will act in the face of these issues.

Having looked at the external context it is now appropriate to look at the internal context: the organization itself.

ANALYSING THE ORGANIZATION

The second element of situation analysis is the investigation of the organization of the organization. Chapter 2 provides some detail on the types of question that need to be asked when looking at the organization as a whole. It goes almost without saying that any assessment of the organization must be both thorough and honest.

In addition to the areas identified in Chapter 2 that must be analysed, there needs to be an assessment of the organization's performance. Is it good at what it does? What are its aspirations and are they realistic? Also germane is an assessment of the organization's culture – the way it does things and the 'set of conscious and unconscious beliefs, values and patterns of behaviour (including language and symbol use) that provide identity and form a framework of meaning for a group of people'.[1] Is this culture conducive to the achievements of the organization's objectives? Does it align with the expectations of the organization's external stakeholders? An analysis of this will reveal the extent of the internal communications task, although clearly it will also identify issues that may be to do with the organization's structure, processes and practices, which also need to be resolved and which are not amenable to communication solutions alone.

Following this kind of analysis, the public relations planner can begin again to categorize the analysis in a structured way, similar to the way that EPISTLE organizes thinking for external analysis purposes.

One way to approach this is to divide these considerations by undertaking a SWOT analysis. The first two elements, **S**trengths and **W**eaknesses, can be seen as internally driven and particular to the organization. The other two, **O**pportunities and **T**hreats, are normally external and will have been largely identified through the PEST analysis. The four elements can be seen as mirror segments in a quadrant. Below. A brief example follows.

STRENGTHS	WEAKNESSES
Financially strong	Conservative in investment
Innovative	Restricted product line
Good leadership	Traditional and hierarchical
Good reputation	Complacent
Loyal workforce	Inflexible working patterns

OPPORTUNITIES	THREATS
Cheap supplies from Eastern Europe	Reputational issues arising from potential accusations of exploitation
To expand into China	Danger of being overstretched
To acquire competitors	To be taken over by a larger conglomerate

It is sometimes useful to apply SWOT analysis to categories of activity, for example corporate, product, internal and so on.

Again, the purpose of the SWOT analysis is to identify and then prioritize the major issues that face the organization in order to design public relations programmes that will address these issues. By definition, the analysis will identify those issues that have strategic importance since they isolate those areas that have societal and corporate significance for the organization. By addressing those areas, the public relations function will be able to demonstrate its contribution to organizational effectiveness.

A legitimate question might be why should the public relations person be involved in all this external and internal research, after all their business is relationship building through communication? It is precisely because this is their business, that practitioners need to be alert to the drivers affecting an organization – probably as much if not more than anyone else in the organization. The purpose of having a public relations function is to help an organization meet its objectives. If a public relations professional is not aware of the drivers that frame company objectives, how can he or she fulfil the boundary-spanning communication role described earlier (see Chapter 1)?

Taking the above analysis into consideration we can see from the SWOT example that the public relations programme will have a number of jobs to do in support of corporate objectives. For example, to mount a marketing communications campaign if the product line is to be expanded. An internal communications programme will be needed to assist in managing change. An international corporate and government relations campaign will be required to support expansion into China, and a financial relations programme will certainly be needed to preserve a strong reputation, raise capital to fund expansion and offset takeover possibilities.

Having determined from an organizational point of view what the key issues are and the organization's stance on them, it is then the public relations professional's job to create a public relations programme with objectives that address those issues.

ANALYSING THE STAKEHOLDER

The third element of situation analysis is to investigate the current state of stakeholder and publics' attitudes, opinions and behaviours towards the organization.

Smith[2] calls this 'analysing public perception' and says there are two elements to this:

Visibility: that is the extent to which the organization is known. Do people know about it? What do they know and is this accurate?

Reputation: how do people regard the organization? Their perceptions will be based on 'the verbal, visual and behavioural messages, both planned and unplanned, that come from an organization' (see page 33).

If an organization has good visibility and a strong reputation, it will be easier to build on this. If it does not, then the reverse is true.

Lerbinger[3] calls the type of research that defines stakeholders and publics and finds out how they perceive an organization before, during and after a campaign 'public relations audits'. If the view that stakeholders have of an organization differs from the reality, there is an issue that needs to be addressed. The problem may be lack of information, or wrong information, that can be countered quite easily. The problem might be more profound or complex, for example, the organization might have a reputation for being a bad employer because it had to make 50 per cent of its workforce redundant to survive several years before and the legacy lingers on.

Then the task is to discover if a real communication problem exists, what the actual problem is, with whom (which stakeholders), what needs to be communicated, how it should be communicated and whether or not there has been effective communication in the past. Lerbinger[3] calls the kind of research that evaluates whether or not content has got through to the targeted publics 'communications audits'. 'Social audits' research the consequences of an organization's actions on its publics and monitor corrective actions; this kind of research may need to be done before a campaign starts, particularly if the campaign is required as a result of organizational action that has had an adverse effect, as is often the case in crises. Once again, detailed research into stakeholders and publics will reveal any issues that need to be addressed.

It can be seen that detailed investigation into internal and external environments and of stakeholders and publics is required in order to obtain a complete understanding of the issues that need to be addressed. Issues then need to be drawn together, examined to see where there are linkages, and prioritized according to the extent to which they either enable or block the organization achieving its objectives now or into the future. These issues then form the *raison d'être* of specific public relations programmes. Figure 4.2 shows the process and an example of how these issues can be linked.

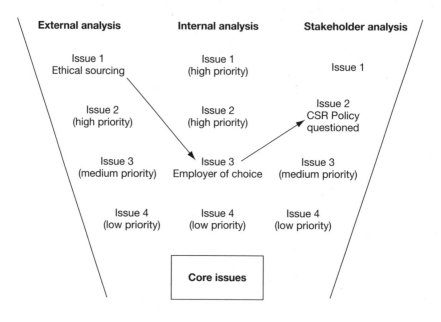

Figure 4.2 *Prioritizing and linking issues*

In this example the organization understands that there are external societal pressures which increasingly require that companies should ensure that they source their raw materials ethically – wood from sustainable forests, cloth produced by companies that do not employ child labour, etc. They also identify that although quite well respected as an employer, they are not the employer of choice by graduates. Their stakeholder analysis also reveals that there are questions about their corporate responsibility commitments, possibly because they have had suspect environmental policies in the past. It is clear that there are linkages between these issues and that they should have a high priority. A core issue for them and one in which public relations may play a key role in bringing it to the attention of senior management, is to address the area of sustainable sourcing, which could then make them both an employer of choice and address some of their stakeholder concerns on their corporate social responsibility (CSR) policies. However, without this detailed analysis they would not have a rounded picture of the issue, neither would they understand the extent to which it affects the reputation and potential relationship of the organization, or of the potential benefits they would achieve by tackling it.

Although research around the topic in hand needs to be rigorous and objective, it need not necessarily be expensive – it depends on the task. If what is needed to find out the views of the local community, it is a simple matter to walk the streets and ask, to go to the local cafes, to ask local community groups (actual and virtual) and to speak to local community leaders. This might be all that is required. If, however, the task is to launch a major campaign aimed at changing the country's eating habits, much more detailed and sophisticated research will be required.

The principles behind formative research are the same whether they are for major, strategic, long-term programmes or short campaigns. Research helps to establish what the real issues are and the nature and size of the public relations task.

WHO SHOULD UNDERTAKE THE RESEARCH?

Given that whole programmes or campaigns are based on research, it is important that it is carried out properly. It is not good enough to instruct the most junior member of the public relations team to contact a few customers to find out what they think of the existing corporate identity. Those involved in serious research must be trained. Getting biased or incomplete answers will lead to ill-founded programmes. There are several excellent short courses and textbooks on conducting research. Investment is needed to become competent at collecting basic information and interpreting it accurately and fully, but this need not cost a fortune.

Obviously, an established research consultancy or trained in-house people will know all about undertaking valid research, which involves, for example, selecting a sample that genuinely reflects the universe being studied.

Sometimes it is entirely legitimate to do a 'quick and dirty' study of, for example, reactions of personal finance journalists to a new pension plan, as long as limitations of that study are recognized and it is not used as anything other than a fairly superficial survey of a very particular group of people.

The benefits of using trained in-house researchers are that they know the business and will need little briefing except for the specifics of the research problem. On the downside, they may be seen to be less objective than external researchers.

External researchers could very well offer skills in specialized research areas, including communication. They may be perceived to be more objective, but are often (although not necessarily) more expensive because they build in learning time, overheads, profits and so on.

Of course, it is perfectly possible to mix the two: internal administration and collection of results, with professional advice on questionnaire design, with a research company analysing the results for you.

It is worth bearing in mind that interpretation of results is critically important and if savings have to be made, it is advisable not to make them here.

RESEARCH TECHNIQUES

Quantitative, qualitative, mixed and tracking research

There are several different types of research. First of all there is quantitative research which collects data that is then expressed statistically giving results in numbers or quantities, and there is qualitative research, which investigates non-quantifiable variables such as opinions, reactions and attitudes. Thus, measuring how many people have blue, green or brown eyes or who will vote for a particular party at a general election is quantitative research; finding out what views an individual has on the policies of the major political parties is qualitative research.

Many situations require a mixture of qualitative and quantitative methods. The public relations planner needs to know how many people are involved, what their attitude or behaviour is, and why. Segmentation is used to group people with similar characteristics together. This reveals how many are in the group and what their key attitudinal and behavioural drivers are.

Continuous or tracking research is where the same group of people or people of the same profile are asked the same questions at regular intervals. Building societies regularly survey groups of people on a one-off basis, but with the same characteristics, to find out what awareness of the various societies is. Advertising and public relations research companies track stakeholder awareness of communication: what they recall and how they interpret it etc. Satisfaction surveys track whether or not customers are happy with the performance of a company, product or service over time.

The large research companies frequently conduct Omnibus surveys to discover all kinds of things, from views on the economy to opinions on executive pay. Surveys are undertaken on just about anything from food preferences to what people thought of various countries performance in the last football World Cup.

Continuous or tracking surveys are particularly helpful when trying to measure something like consumer trends or changes in attitude over time.

One-off surveys are useful if factual information on which to establish a campaign is needed. For example, what proportion of the population buys wigs and who they are will need to be known before a new kind of wig is launched.

Primary and secondary research

Information can be collected in two ways: via primary or secondary research. Secondary research is often called desk research and entails collecting information from already published sources. There is an enormous amount of published data that can be accessed. The trick is knowing where to find it. Public and university libraries have vast collections of material on companies and industry sectors, social trends and so on and they are often connected to international information databases. They also have newspapers and magazines archived on virtual and hard copy databases and CD ROM, as do trade libraries run by professional bodies such as the Law Society. Government departments hold statistics on subjects relevant to them and the National Statistics Office in the UK holds an enormous bank of information. Company reports and corporate and product literature are available from most organizations. Almost everything under the sun has been surveyed at some stage and most libraries are happy to point researchers in the right direction. The internet also provides huge possibilities for obtaining information from individuals, aggregators and organizations worldwide and the use of various search engines to identify and aggregate information is an invaluable resource. Several research companies are capitalizing on the almost insatiable appetite for information. It is essential for the public relations professional to bear in mind that many journalists, especially the specialists, use the internet as their primary information source and understanding their sources of information is vital.

The large research companies such as Mintel, IPSOS-MORI and Gallup conduct their own surveys on various topics, and listings are available so that their reports can be bought very easily, either as hard copy or electronically. Of course desk research takes time and hiring the services of a professional researcher could make the task much easier if time means money. However, research that has already been conducted is often a great deal cheaper than doing the work from scratch. A quick call or an e-mail and a small fee to a research organization to find out what's available could save a great deal of money.

The benefits of secondary research are that it is available quickly, it is usually more comprehensive and cheaper than doing it personally and it provides a basis on which to conduct further specific research if necessary. Some of the problems with secondary sources are that the quality is sometimes suspect, the quantity can be overwhelming and integrating data from

different sources can be difficult. It is also not tailored to particular requirements.

Primary research is finding out the information at first hand by going
directly to the source. There are various empirical techniques for obtaining
primary data, some of which are listed below.

Self-completion questionnaires

These are a relatively cheap way to contact a large number of people over a
geographically widespread area (or even a small number of people in a
geographically tight area). They are excellent for obtaining information
from people who are difficult to contact (maybe they are shift workers) and
they allow time for people to consider their answers carefully before
responding. It is useful to include an incentive (for example, free entry to a
prize draw) to encourage a good response. Self-completion questionnaires
need to be clear, simple and as short as possible. They can be distributed
and collected by post, in person or via another medium such as the internet
or a magazine, and are usually completed by the respondent without supervision. If a questionnaire is more complex it can be issued to groups, with a
trained researcher supervising the session or answering questions that may
arise.

Questionnaires are often used to obtain a mass of quantitative data, but
can also be used for qualitative material. Good questionnaires that are unbi-
ased, unambiguous and which collect all the information that is required
are very difficult to design. Professional help must often be sought from
trained researchers.

One-to-one depth interviews

This survey technique is excellent for collecting qualitative data. Interviews
are obviously time consuming for the researcher and the interviewee, and
this method is very expensive if a mass of data is required. There are ways
in which the costs of interviewing can be kept down. It is relatively cheap to
participate in an omnibus survey which may be run by one of the larger
research organizations. They often undertake regular surveys on specific
groups such as teenagers and industry sectors like motoring, and on particular products such as computer games. A few questions can be added to the
survey and they charge per question. Results from these interviews can
usually be turned around very quickly, often with a few days.

There are also syndicated studies where the results are available to those
who subscribe to the service. The survey mentioned earlier where building
societies track awareness is a syndicated study with the participating building societies obtaining the results for a fee. These omnibus or syndicated

studies are more suited to quantitative questions, but it is possible to ask a few, very well crafted qualitative questions that will require explicit interpretation.

Although relatively expensive, the quality and quantity of information that can be gathered from tailor-made one-to-one interviews can be superb. Again it is important to stress that interviewing is a particular skill and training is required to get the best from the opportunity. Interviews can be structured so that specific information is collected, unstructured where the questions are developed as a result of the answers given, or somewhere in between – semi-structured.

Interviewing allows the researcher to explore views and opinions in depth, and the reasons why those views are held. When trying to get to the heart of difficult issues it is an excellent technique to use. Sophisticated computer programs are now available to analyse text, picking out key words and phrases, and facilitate quantitative as well as qualitative analysis.

Telephone interviews

This technique is particularly suitable for collecting structured information. They are a kind of halfway house between face-to-face interviews and questionnaires. They don't allow as much probing as the face-to-face interview or the reflection of the questionnaire, but they are a relatively speedy way to collect information from a broad or narrow section of respondents. The Computer Aided Telephone Interview (CATI) system allows researchers to input answers to questions very quickly and instant analysis is possible. CATI systems also provide call management facilities such as organizing calls, redialling engaged numbers and keeping statistics of failed contacts. A danger of this technique is that many people resent the intrusion of telephone research, particularly when at home, and the data gathered can be biased with the respondent giving answers to satisfy the researcher or in an unconsidered way to get the researcher 'off the phone'.

Focus groups

Focus groups are discussion groups comprising carefully selected individuals (maybe with the same profile, for example 20- to 25-year-old Asian women, married with children, all born in the UK and living in Cardiff; or maybe of the same age, gender and location, but with very different backgrounds). Running a successful focus group is a highly skilled activity and requires a competent co-ordinator to guide discussion and to ensure all the relevant questions are asked. The idea behind a focus group is that the responses from the participants prompt and develop responses from other participants. Properly done, focus groups can obtain far more information than one-to-one interviews. There are difficulties associated with this technique: selection of participants, length of time needed, facilities required (room, recording equipment), expense (travel costs, refreshments), danger of bias, particularly if there is a participant who is persuasive of others, but the depth of insight that can be acquired is a rich reward.

Internet groups

As well as gathering information from various sources on the internet, it is very easy to undertake one-to-one or group research. For example, visitors to a website can be asked to fill in a short questionnaire or to make comments on particular subjects. Bulletin boards or chat rooms can be hosted on a site. A viral campaign could drive traffic to a particular site or forum for discussion and comment. Twitter is also a good source for instant and 'quick and dirty' research that may provide insight into more extensive work that needs to be undertaken, but it should never be regarded as proper, scientific evidence since it is a self-selecting community and could not be replicated.

The use of e-mail, intranets and extranets means that contacting and obtaining the views of specific groups of people, for example employees or suppliers, is simple and fast. Of course, the temptation to go back to these sources repeatedly (to the point of annoyance), because it is so easy, must be resisted. On the other hand, the opportunity to set up a genuine and ongoing dialogue with stakeholders in which research is an integral part is something that it would be irresponsible to miss.

Observation

Watching what people do is very enlightening. People can be asked what they do and they can describe it more or less accurately. However, seeing them in context reveals all those things that even they are not aware of, for example, the influence of others, the way in which they work or complete a task, what they find hard or easy to accomplish. Observation can be undertaken over a long or short period of time. For example, anthropologists may live with and observe groups for extended periods to understand their way of life and cultures. Such a level of detail can be invaluable to the public relations practitioner. On the other hand, observing just a few meetings of the CEO with staff will provide enough data to advise him or her on their presentation techniques, and will be far more informative than extended interviews with them and their staff.

Observation can either be non-participant – that is, no part is taken by the researcher, or participant – that is, the researcher will intervene to a greater or lesser extent. For example, they may just ask questions to clarify points, or they may become a fully operational member of the activity or team. Mystery shoppers play the part of a 'proper' consumer, although they may be briefed to enact a particular role, for example, a difficult customer, or one with a specific disability, to test the responses of the objects of the research. In these kinds of cases, careful thought has to be given to the ethics of research: indeed, the ethical conduct of research must be considered in any research programme.

The benefit of primary research is that it can be tailored to the public relations researcher's specific requirements. It can delve into attitudes, opinions and behaviours and answer the question 'why' – a key to understanding communication issues, and essential to decisions about how the researcher would like people to move, either attitudinally or behaviourally. It can fill gaps left by secondary research and it can be used to test initial reactions to ideas and proposals. Its disadvantages are that it is usually more expensive than secondary research, often time-consuming, and it is easy to miss vital questions, which leaves the research incomplete. Problems also arise if the primary research indicates conflicting evidence from secondary research – who has the right answer?

Informal research

Apart from formal research techniques, there are all kinds of informal ways of obtaining information about issues and organizations. Chance encounters and informal discussions with the whole range of publics associated with an organization such as competitors, specialist journalists, neighbours and suppliers can be very enlightening. Getting a feel for the organization by attending its annual general meeting or social events helps. Don't just talk to the obvious people: cleaners, secretaries and security people are very well connected and have a 'sense' for the organization, and are often more honest and realistic than senior people with a vested interest. Regular reading of the press, internet searches, listening to and watching general interest and current affairs programmes, even discussions with friends and colleagues in social situations, help to build an all-embracing overview of the context and the specifics of any particular situation, and help make connections between issues and organizations that might not be available via formal research.

Informal, or 'quick and dirty' research, has its value. A very successful campaign to save a London hospital was based on the public relations executive walking the streets surrounding the hospital asking people about it and talking to people in the pub. Not a procedure recommended as exemplary, but time was pressing and it provided essential information about the strength of local feeling from a broad spectrum of people.

Media research

It is important not only to know the organization and the relevant issues, but to investigate the channels of communication too. The written and broadcast media provide information on readership profiles, circulation, effectiveness of advertising, reaction to copy and so on. Organizations such as Technorati do the same for the internet. Other media such as direct mail, advertising, posters and sponsorship can also be analysed. The various media have their own trade bodies that can provide detailed information on their use and effectiveness, and this should be carefully considered when deciding which channels should be used for particular publics.

Communication audit

Apart from researching the issues affecting an organization or the facts surrounding a particular campaign, it is vitally important for the public relations professional to examine in detail the communication process itself. This is done via a communication audit. In brief, a communication audit identifies those publics vital to an organization's success. It investigates the scope of communication to determine whether all existing or potential publics are being covered. It examines their current attitudes and behaviours to assess whether or not work is required to confirm or change them and what other engagement is required. It appraises critically the nature and quality of the communication between the organization and its publics, looking carefully at the content that is being relayed to see if it is what is required, its frequency and the techniques that are used to transmit it, as well as the effectiveness of the communication. It identifies communication gaps and unexploited opportunities, as well as the information needs of all the key publics. It also looks ahead by examining future information requirements and new methods of communication that should be used. An audit also pinpoints the resources and skills needed to run a successful programme or campaign, and whether or not these are available to an organization.

To undertake an effective audit requires extensive research of the organization's context; within an organization, with the whole range of personnel responsible for communication, and with the stakeholders and publics of the organization to investigate the opinions of those who are in contact with it.

Interpreting the findings

Collecting data can be a complex task but what should be done with it once it has been obtained? At the risk of becoming repetive, it is important to stress that analysing and interpreting data is a highly skilled job. All too often very simple analysis is done on very rich data. Obvious conclusions are drawn from statistics when analysed by the statistically illiterate. It could be that 24 per cent of your sample said no to your questions, 49 per cent said yes, but 26 per cent said maybe. It is true that most people said yes, but the majority said either no or maybe and they may be more inclined to no rather than yes. There is no clear confirmation of a positive answer. It could well be that enlightenment will come from using information from other parts of the survey, but more detailed investigation may be required. The golden rule is: once having paid good money for research ensure full interpretation and professional help may be required for that.

INVESTMENT IN RESEARCH PAYS – TWO CASES IN POINT

The point of doing research is to enable public relations programmes to be undertaken more effectively. Identifying what the real issues are and the best way to go about executing a programme is, of course, vital to its success.

Research sometimes throws up the unexpected and drives practitioners to conduct programmes in a way that might not have been anticipated. This is good news because if programmes are conducted on hunches, rather than the way that research dictates, the end result is wasted time, effort and money, and not achieving or at best only partially achieving your objectives. An example of how research guided a campaign is given below.

Love Food, Hate Waste, conducted by Trimedia on behalf of WRAP (Waste and Resources Action Programme)

Research undertaken by WRAP in 2007 had established that 6.7 million tonnes of food waste is generated in UK homes every year and, without action, the figure was set to increase into the future. The research also showed that a third of all food purchased was thrown away, most of which could have been eaten. Astoundingly, consumers were unaware of food waste as an economic issue, and 90 per cent of them claimed not to waste food. Once alerted to the problem, they were keen to do something about it.

The big task then, was to work with consumers, owners of food brands and retailers to connect them with the issue of food waste and to stop it reaching landfill sites. In response to the task, Trimedia devised Love Food, Hate Waste (LFHW), the world's first campaign encouraging consumers to reduce food waste in the home. The whole campaign was based on a major piece of research that examined consumer attitudes and behaviours towards food and an exhaustive analysis of food waste.

Client Objectives

The client (WRAP) had four objectives:

- raise awareness of food waste and the LFHW campaign;
- encourage consumers to review their own attitudes and behaviour;
- work with WRAP to reduce the amount of food going to landfill sites by 100,000 tonnes, by summer 2008;
- provide a solution to the problem and a means to access these solutions.

Target audience

- all consumers, but especially families and 'foodies'.

Strategy

There was a three-step approach to the campaign:

- use 'shocking facts' to grab consumers' attention;
- personalize the campaign so that consumers engage with the issue;
- use a variety of 'enabling tools' to help people change their behaviour towards food waste.

Planning

The factors associated with food waste and our relationship with food is complex, as the research showed (see Figure 4.3). A simple, glib approach just telling people to cut down on waste would not be at all appropriate. To add complexity, this type of campaign had not been undertaken before and responses to it were very difficult to predict. How would consumers react? Would there be opposition from consumer groups and food producers? Would it be seen as another example of the 'nanny state' preaching to the public? Again, a deep understanding of consumers' relationship to food, gained through the research, was critical to getting the content and the tone of the campaign right.

Bearing all these issues in mind and the need for sustained engagement post campaign launch, and partnership working, an intense four-stage media campaign was planned to establish LFHW as a campaign and as a brand. All the stages were underpinned by careful research and testing.

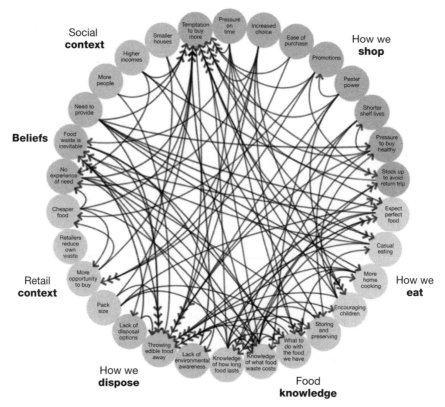

Figure 4.3 *The complex relationship with food*

Action

The key tactics employed were:

Stage 1: Pre-launch

Based on research into food wastage, a number of editorial ideas were developed for the key media, highlighting the 'shocking facts' about waste. This was complemented by a range of practical ways to reduce waste so that consumers could take action.

Some of the 'shocking facts' were:

- £3 billion is wasted on good food that is thrown away: that is £430 per person every year;
- 5.1 million potatoes, 4.4 million apples, 2.8 million tomatoes, 1.6 million bananas and 1.2 million oranges – all perfectly wholesome – are thrown away every year;
- one in three bags of food purchased ends up being thrown away.

Solutions that were proposed included:

- keeping fruit in the fridge;
- using up leftovers;
- better portion control;
- home composting.

Some of the complex and potentially conflicting issues related to waste were also carefully thought through. For example, the government is also encouraging five portions of fresh fruit and vegetables a day and ironically it is vegetables and fruit that is wasted most. Care had to be taken not to blame families for wanting to eat healthily and much of the advice and practical guidance therefore focused on storage and use rather than on discouraging good eating habits. There were also ready and controversial discussion points on supermarket practices, such as buy one, get one free offers, which can encourage people to purchase more than they need, but undoubtedly also encourage people to eat more vegetables.

Stage 2: Recruiting supporters

Recognized food industry experts were identified through research and recruited to the campaign, including Caroline Mason, ex-cookery editor of *Good Housekeeping* magazine, who helped with recipes and in offering practical solutions to the problems of food waste. Award-winning journalist and broadcaster Richard Johnson helped to recruit chefs. The majority of the UK's leading chefs and food writers gave their support and a Love Food champion's community project was initiated with the Women's Institute, who provided practical advice and feedback from local communities.

Stage 3: The launch of LFHW

Launch day was staged at London Borough Market, a venue synonymous with the campaign's values. Thirty journalists, crews and key stakeholders heard from WRAP CEO Liz Goodwin, Environment Minister Joan Ruddock and Richard Johnson. Celebrity chefs Ainsley Harriot, Paul Merrit and Barry Haughton acted as campaign advocates to provide mainstream and 'foodie' appeal. Cook-offs and web stations showing an information-packed and advice-filled website, provided the interactive elements and a show reel of chefs and celebrities who all gave their time for free was played. This not only brought the practical advice to life, but also brought emotional depth and personal connections to the issue.

Stage 4: Maintaining momentum

After the launch it was imperative to ensure the campaign stayed in the front of consumers' minds. To help sustain and embed the campaign, the following happened:

- BBC *Good Food Show* regional radio show was a crucial exercise to meet a 'warm foodie' audience through a LFHW stand. This was successful, demonstrating both that the media were interested in the food-waste debate and that there was a receptive consumer audience keen to understand the issues and reduce food waste in their homes.
- A Christmas to February campaign focusing on the 230,000 tonnes of festive food waste, worth some £275 million, providing new stories, tips on leftovers and advice on making meals go further.
- An April burst, focusing on fruit and vegetable waste using the banner 'an apple a day gets thrown away', to highlight the 4.4 million apples that are discarded daily.

- In May, launching the research-based Food We Waste report to media and stake-holders, which for the first time in the UK identified how much food in their various categories we waste – from whole chickens and yoghurts, to cans of lager and chocolate gateaux.

Evaluation

The results of the campaign demonstrated significant success:

- 555 pieces of coverage (Objective 1);
- 100 per cent penetration of key media, with 99 per cent of all print coverage favourable and 98 per cent including at least one core message (Objective 1);
- 43 leading chefs, foodies, journalists and celebrities have actively contributed to the campaign, free of charge (Objective 1);
- 1.45 million households have committed to throwing away less food (Objective 2);
- this will lead to a reduction of 500,000 of carbon dioxide equivalents (Objective 2); and
- translates into savings for consumers of almost £240 million (Objective 2);
- the figures above reflect a reduction of food waste going to landfill of some 100,000 tonnes (Objective 3);
- 154,000 people visited and contributed to the LFHW website (Objective 4);
- 54 per cent of all print coverage included practical advice (Objective 4);

Budget

The campaign cost £150,000.

Points about the campaign

- This was the first time food waste was the subject of such a campaign, so potentially high risk. Careful research and close working with respected industry figures and stakeholders helped reduce the risk.
- The campaign was based on solid research that could not be refuted: about the facts of food waste, our relationship with food, consumer habits, industry practices, practical solutions, and this yielded a deep insight of the kind of facts that would connect with consumers without prompting an adverse reaction.
- The campaign clearly lent itself to a staged roll-out. Critical to success was obtaining prior buy-in from key individuals and organizations and both WRAP and Trimedia spent time collecting and testing information that then could be used during the campaign.
- There was a successful follow-up to the launch. A danger was always that it would run out of steam, but the team showed the constraint and judgement of not putting everything into the launch.
- The raft of tactics was relatively limited, but they were impactful because they focused on deep engagement: necessary where behaviour change is required.
- The mix of rational and emotional appeal was very good. The 'killer' facts were simple and easy to grasp, while being shocking, but there was also a range of solutions readily available to capitalise on both the rational and emotional response. In other words, the campaign covered all the bases.

Research can be used not only strategically to underpin a whole programme, but also as a specific tool for implementing a public relations campaign. Here the approach is quite overt. A certain topic is researched for its media appeal and the findings used in the campaign, either all at once or on a phased basis. A virtue may be made of undertaking the research regularly and announcing the results, for example the Nationwide Building Society researches house prices and produces its house-price survey on a regular monthly basis.

Credibility can be added by enlisting the services of a well-known and respected research agency to undertake the work. Indeed, one of the more sure-fire media 'hooks' is to base a media campaign on research. The magical words are 'A survey has revealed…'. If that research touches on matters of public interest, it can serve a useful social purpose as well as obtaining publicity. The following example demonstrates how such research can be used.

'Snorers' Sleep-in' conducted by Trimedia Belgium for GlaxoSmithKline

Background

Snoring is a serious problem for individuals and their partners, causing distress to both, and in serious cases leading to conflict. Breathe Right Nasal Strips, made by GlaxoSmithKline helps to reduce or eliminate snoring.

To mark the re-launch of Breathe Right anti-snoring nose strips in Belgium, GlaxoSmithKline asked Trimedia to develop an attention-grabbing campaign.

Strategy

Trimedia's strategy was to put snoring on the national agenda by combining visually creative media ideas with scientific research and hence gain visibility for Breathe Right nasal strips.

Implementation

Trimedia combined the results of an international snoring survey, commissioned by GlaxoSmithKline – which showed that 40 per cent of the population of Belgium snores – with a creative event which facilitated direct interaction with both the media and members of the target audience. It was timed to coincide with the International Day of Sleep.

Trimedia invited 10 heavy snorers and their partners to participate in the 'Snorers' Sleep-in' experiment, at the prestigious White Hotel in Brussels, on the eve of International Day of Sleep.

A press conference featured a Breathe Right spokesperson and two independent snoring experts; medical doctor Dr Philippe Rombaux PhD and Dr E Hamans. It was important to obtain third-party, medical endorsement for the experiment. Over lunch, radio and TV interviews were given by the client, the experts and the snorers themselves.

In the evening, Trimedia organized dinner for all participants in the experiment, so they were able to share their snoring experiences with each other, the experts, the client and the media. After dinner, the snorers were invited to a 'Sleep-In', where their snoring levels were measured all night long by a decibel meter. They were observed by independent medical staff and constantly monitored by a nightvision camera from a TV crew who stayed for the duration of the experiment. Each of the snorers' partners were offered a snore free night in a separate, designer room of the hotel!

The snoring level in the snoring suite went up to 77 decibels, (very loud in comparison to the World Health Organization's recommended noise level in a sleeping room of approximately 45 decibels). The snorers were then offered Breathe Right anti-snoring nasal strips as a part of the solution for their snoring problem, and it worked. The results were validated by the medical staff who were observing.

This event captured the imagination of Belgium's national media, leading to widespread coverage and impacted on sales of Breathe Right nasal strips.

Results

The Snorers' Sleep-in was a media hit and resulted in widespread coverage including primetime national television news.

- Print press: 29 clippings; AV Media: 7 radios and 3 TV slots.

Because of the interactivity, the event also resulted in extremely positive feedback from participants and their partners.

This case shows how scientific research can be used effectively with the media, not only to start it off, but as part of a media event itself.

Notes

1. McCollum, M (1997) The culture of work organizations, *Academy of Management Review*, **19**, 836–39.
2. Smith, R D (2009) Strategic Planning for Public Relations (3rd edition), Lawrence Erlbaum Associates, Mahwah, NJ.
3. Lerbinger, O (1972) *Designs for Persuasive Communication*, Prentice Hall, Englewood Cliffs, NJ.

5

Communication theory and setting aims and objectives

KNOWING WHERE YOU'RE GOING

Setting realistic aims and objectives is absolutely vital if the programme or campaign that is being planned is to have direction and demonstrably achieve something.

One of the things that is rife in the public relations industry is poor objective-setting, specifically over-promising. This applies to both in-house departments and consultancies. It comes partly from an eagerness to please, but largely from a lack of knowledge about what can actually be achieved.

Ultimately the aim of public relations is to influence levels of awareness (ie what is thought about something), attitudes or opinions (ie what is felt about something) or behaviour (ie what is done about something). The objective might be to encourage someone to buy a newly introduced furniture range, or keep their holdings in a company, or to speak up for the company when it is under attack, or to support nursery provision even if the target group doesn't have children. However, there are several steps along the way to influen-cing awareness, attitudes or opinions and behaviour and it is only very occasionally that someone who is dedicated to opposing something or who has no particular opinion at all will suddenly become an ardent supporter.

ATTITUDE IS ALL IMPORTANT

Of course one of the things formative research will have shown is whether stakeholders or publics are aware of an organization. It may appear that by definition they should be, but not everyone that the organization does or will affect will be aware of them. For example, a supermarket may intend to open a new store, but will everyone be aware of that intention or of the impact it will have on them? Usually, stakeholders or publics are aware or not aware of an organization, that is quite simple, yes or no. Attitudes or opinions are more complex. Exactly what the attitudes of various stakeholders and publics are will have been investigated during the formative research stage. Attitudes and opinions are complex and will probably have been built up over time and from a variety of sources and experiences. Knowing exactly what attitudes and opinions stakeholders and publics have provides a benchmark measure of the task in hand and this is vitally important when planning a programme. It is a much easier and less time-consuming job to reinforce favourable opinion than to neutralize hostile ones. In fact it may be that it has to be admitted that it is impossible to neutralize ingrained opinions, particularly if they are based on deep-seated prejudice.

So, how are attitudes formed? All kinds of influences impact on people:

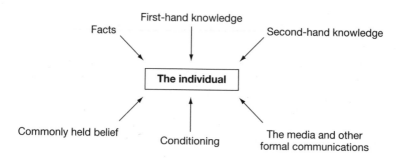

- *First-hand knowledge* is a very powerful attitude former. If a car is bought from a certain garage and the car itself, the sales and after-sales service has been excellent, then the purchaser will have a favourable attitude towards it.

- *Second-hand knowledge* is also a strong influence, particularly if gained from a friend, trusted colleague or an authority of some kind. If an individual hears from a friend about a certain country that knowledge, coupled with good ratings on a consumer website and a good brochure, may persuade us to holiday there.
- *The on-and off-line media* is a potent influence, particularly if a topic is one of heightened public interest such as the concern over standards in public life. Companies also communicate via other formal methods such as annual reports, websites and product literature.
- *Conditioning* influences the way people look at everything they come into contact with. How they have been brought up, their education, religious beliefs, political views, age, sex and social position are all part of the baggage people bring with them when thinking about any subject.
- Then there are *commonly held beliefs.* For example, people may believe, even though they may not own one or know anyone who does, that Aston Martins are superb cars or that Italian suits are especially well designed and made.
- *Facts* also affect attitudes. Knowledge that New Zealand is at the other side of the world will make us disbelieve anyone who says that they can cycle there in half an hour.

Usually attitudes are formed via a combination of all these factors. Some attitudes are very firmly fixed, like views of the service received from a bank, while other attitudes may be much more loosely held, for example views of the Canadian government (in fact most British people may not have an attitude towards the Canadian government at all, but just an awareness that one exists).

THE COMMUNICATION CHAIN

To set realistic objectives, apart from understanding what the attitudes of various stakeholders and publics are, there also needs to be an understand the communication process. Assumptions along the lines of 'If I tell it loud and long and they hear it, eventually they'll believe it' are naive in the extreme. There are several models describing communication between individuals, groups and the main media. Just a few are outlined here to indicate the complexity of the subject.

Real communication involves the two-way exchange of information. However, many public relations practitioners in effect still believe that the one-way, linear communication model whose underlying principles were formulated by Shannon and Weaver[1] in 1949 is what happens in real life. The underlying pattern of the model is like this:

SENDER ⟶ MESSAGE ⟶ CHANNEL ⟶ RECEIVER

The idea is that the sender is active, the receiver is passive and that the message is somehow decanted into the receiver's mind through a channel of communication and that it will be fully understood. Furthermore, no distinction is drawn between communicating with individuals, groups, mass audiences or via third parties.

The above model could apply to individuals, but what's missing is any notion of feedback. Senders need to know if the message has affected the receiver at all by receivers making them aware of something changing or reinforcing attitudes, or making him or her behave in a particular way. For example, the sender could leave a note (channel) saying that dinner is in the oven (message), but they will never know whether the receiver has understood or acted on the message unless they tell the sender or if the dinner is eaten. Feedback closes the loop. A much more realistic model is the fairly well-known one shown in Figure 5.1.

The underlying principles behind this model were developed by Osgood and presented by Schramm[2] in 1954.

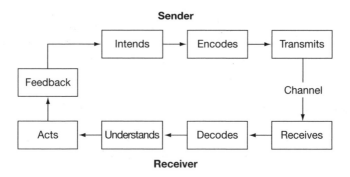

Figure 5.1 *The communication process model*

The sender intends to communicate and articulates or encodes that intention, bringing with him or her all the conditioning baggage mentioned before. He or she then chooses a channel through which to transmit the communication. This may be the spoken word, a letter or a text message or a gesture, and the recipient receives that communication.

The actual transmission of information is fraught with danger. It may be that the message has associated channel noise. The radio may be crackly, the writing may be poorly laid out and hard to read, the receiving mobile phone may be in a poor reception spot, or the website may be difficult to navigate. There may also be psychological noise. The sender might be using the wrong body language or the corporate message from the chief executive may be intimidating rather than informative. Then there is language noise, where the language itself can be misinterpreted. 'Do not cross while light is flashing' can mean do not cross when the light is flashing or do not cross until the light is flashing.

Having once received the message, the recipient then needs to decode it so that it can be understood. He or she also brings all his or her conditioning into the decoding equation. There is then normally some sort of action following on from the communication, which might be encoded or explicit. For example, this might be a simple grunt of recognition or a positive and vehement written rejection of the idea proposed, accompanied by threats. This action then has to be decoded by the receiver and acts as feedback. The loop is then closed, since the sender is looking for a reaction to the message that demonstrates communication has taken place. This allows the possibility of the sender adapting either his or her message or way of communicating, to help understanding and enhance communication or maybe deciding to escalate conflict or to discontinue contact. An important feature of this model is that the sender and receiver are seen as essentially equal and both are involved in encoding, decoding and interpreting. This, in fact, has led to some criticism of the model: it intimates a feeling of equality between the communicating parties. However, observation demonstrates this is not the case, there are sometimes large differences in motivation, power and resources between the participants, although the internet is reducing the capability of the advantaged party to wield that advantage.

More recent models of communication have emphasized the cyclical nature of the process. Rogers and Kincaid[3] developed the 'convergence' model (see Figure 5.2), in which the participants in communication give and receive information and explore their understanding of it to the point where there is a level of mutual understanding (which does not need to be complete) that further exchanges are not necessary. Of course, it is doubtful that complete understanding is ever obtained, but the notion is that there is sufficient understanding of each other's position to be able to make reasonable judgements.

In this model concepts such as the sender, message, receiver are superceded by concepts such as participants, joint activity and joint understanding, where the beginning and end of the process are less clear and who initiated it becomes less important.

The models so far are particularly applicable to one-to-one, interpersonal communication, where there can be relatively easy checks on understanding and where there is feedback, for example, one-to-one briefings. They are less suitable as descriptions of what happens between organizations and groups or between organizations and mass audiences or groups reached through a third party such as the media, where there can be relatively little feedback or direct personal interaction.

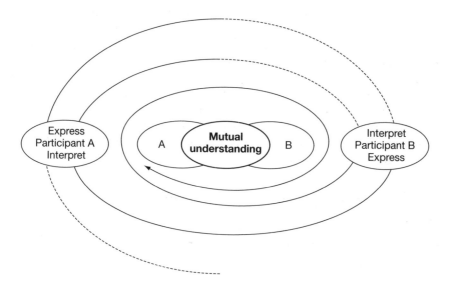

Figure 5.2   *The convergence model of communication*

Reprinted with the kind permission of The Free Press, a division of Simon & Schuster Inc, from *Communication Networks: Toward a new paradigm for research* by Everett M Rogers and D Lawrence Kincaid. Copyright ©1981 by The Free Press

Communicating with groups

There are several models available describing communication with groups; one that is quite widely accepted in public relations circles is the 'co-orientation model'.[4] This is particularly applicable where the organization is involved in a genuine dialogue – two-way, interactive communication in which the organization is prepared to change its position to accommodate its publics. It is not applicable where the organization is just giving out pure information or is undertaking a persuasive exercise only.

Without going into the fine detail of the co-orientation model, its principal features are accuracy, understanding and agreement. An example will illustrate the idea. Suppose a company wishes to set up a plastic recycling plant in a town. It thinks it will provide employment, stimulate the local economy and serve a laudable 'green' cause. Local residents, however, may see this development as bringing heavy lorries to the district, polluting the air and taking up space that could be used for much-needed housing. Each party may have a quite inaccurate perception of the views of the other; they may not understand each other's point of view and they certainly don't agree.

81

The company, realizing that there is a potential major problem, begins to communicate openly with the residents, explaining its motivations for opening the plant. The residents, too, express their reservations. Through the process of discussion, more accurate perceptions of each other's position are achieved. Both sides gradually adjust their understanding as they proceed: they co-orient themselves. They may not like the posiiton of the other side, they may agree to disagree, but at least there is common understanding. From this position, the aim would be to discuss how they can compromise and come to a mutually acceptable solution, even if both sides have to give ground in the process.

Communicating with mass audiences or via the mass media

When dealing with mass audiences there are many receivers and it is impossible to influence people in a uniform way. People select information depending on their various states of knowledge or their predisposition. Receivers talk to each other, they are influenced by opinion leaders and so on. This recognition has led to the development of the two-step communication model[5], where the information is received by key 'gatekeepers' (normally opinion leaders), who further interpret for the mass audience.

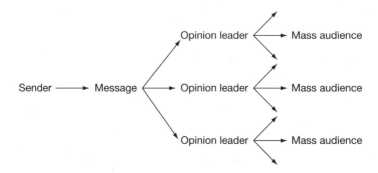

Thus, for example, if a public relations practitioner sends out a press release, the targeted journalists perform the role of opinion leaders and interpret the information on behalf of their readers. Again, some uniformity of interpretation is assumed.

In reality this model is too simplistic. People receive information from all kinds of sources and this often bypasses the opinion leader. Communication is multi-faceted, multi-step and multi-directional.[6]

All this communication is overlaid with individual and group attitudes, psychological variables, channel noise, feedback from various sources and the knowledge base of all those involved. Little wonder, then, that communication with mass audiences is an immensely complex and open-ended business.

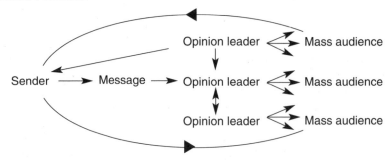

The convergence model given at Figure 5.2 has particular application to communication between individuals, but there are certain principles at play here that also apply to groups. It is essentially a network model because the effect of the communication comes from joint activity and affects all those involved. Network models have a number of features that are important in understanding what is happening in communication:

- Connectedness: an analysis of how highly connected individuals are to a network, will give an indication of how quickly information will flow through it. Highly connected networks are tight communities, whereas more loosely connected networks have members who are more isolated: they may not receive information, or receive it more slowly.
- Integration: this provides an indication of the type and number of linkages between members of the network. So, for example, if members share social networking sites, text, phone and e-mail each other regularly, they have many channels of communication and this can be useful to the public relations practitioner.
- Diversity: if the network is diverse, there will be several routes into the network. If it is not diverse, it will tend to exclude those who do not conform to the characteristics of its membership.
- Openness: if the network is open to external contacts and influences and is well linked to the environment, it will be easier to reach than those that are closed.

By taking into account these features, the public relations practitioner can plan communications better. Through examining the nature of networks the practitioner can also understand why there are blockages in communication: for example, it may be difficult to break into a network because it lacks diversity, thus the only way to enter it is to work with third parties who are acceptable to the membership. For example, activist groups are normally unreceptive to those who do not share their views, hence a way to gain the opportunity to communicate with them is to work with a third party who they may respect as being sympathetic to, or even a member of their network.

Undertaking an analysis of networks forces public relations planners to look at the structure of a whole network and is particularly useful when looking at web-based communities. It reveals information about the membership of the network. There will be individuals who fulfil the liaison role – they link individuals or clusters within the network. There will be stars who are linked to large numbers of other individuals. Isolates are linked to very few individuals and boundary-spanners make links to the wider environment. Bridge individuals create links between the group and other groups, whereas non-participants just get on with their work without communicating. They may, for example, set up links to other websites, which just 'appear', without telling everyone they have done this.

Recognizing these roles enables planners to understand how communication will move around a network. Stars are the planners' friend (or enemy), since they are very well connected and will have great reach into the network. Isolates may need particular attention since information may not reach them and they in turn will not pass it on to many others in the network. Bridges will be ideal for passing information from one network to another.

Network analysis can be used as a tool to understand how information flows around a particular community. Networking itself can be used as a communication strategy. Linking in to particular networks can be the most effective and authoritative way of connecting with certain groups, especially those who are hard to reach. It has been used to great effect by Cumbria County Council, when handling the difficulties surrounding the Appleby Horse Fair.

The Annual Appleby Horse Fair is an unofficial event held in the northern town of Appleby in the UK. Every year, Travellers meet to renew friendships and trade horses: highly symbolic and useful animals in the Traveller's life. There is a tense relationship between the residents of Appleby whose town is filled with Travellers during the week of the fair. Residents complain of drunkenness, litter and other anti-social behaviour. Travellers on the other hand, believe their traditional way of life is becoming increasingly threatened and do not want to see the Fair banned, which was an option being considered by the Council.

By undertaking a careful analysis of the Traveller community – their way of life; membership of their network; who the influencers are inside and outside; how the network operates (stars, bridges and boundary-spanners) – Cumbria County Council were able to plan a communications campaign that put clear boundaries around acceptable and unacceptable behaviours, explain the facilities that were available for use by the Travelling community and open up avenues for contact if any issues arose that needed to be discussed. They then used the network itself as the primary means of communicating these things. The result was that in 2008, local residents congratulated the Council on the best ever Appleby Horse Fair and relations between the three parties – residents, Travellers and Council – were greatly improved.

Communication implications of the internet age

These discussions on public relations theories lead to a number of conclusions:

- Transparent, two-way, proactive and interactive public relations is the only sensible way to operate: there are too many other sources of information to permit any alternative to transparency. In addition, being seen to be a useful information resource and providing transparent access is regarded as a positive indicator of social responsibility.
- Publics can be seen as collecting around issues rather than as homogeneous blocks such as 'customers'. Furthermore, because issues can remain on websites or social networks for prolonged periods, the choice of when to react is in the hands of publics. Issues can re-emerge at any stage, maybe years later, as different groups of people gather round the issue and form a 'new' public. (See Chapter 6 for more detail on issues-based publics.)
- The internet is the friend of *active* and *aware* publics, who are information-seekers. They are potentially the greatest friends of an organization as well as its greatest 'problems'. (For a full explanation of active and aware publics, see Chapter 6.)
- The thought to action continuum desired by organizational communicators can be reinforced or broken by users accessing alternative information sources, many of which may be unknown to the organization.
- This continuum is time-contracted, as information for decision making is readily and swiftly available. Prompts to action in support of or opposition to an organization can be stimulated when a user is part of a like-minded and supportive community (witness the demonstrations against capitalism at G8 Summits and the opposition activity following the Iranian election in 2009, which were both organized through the internet).
- Lack of information from organizations is a potentially serious problem because there will be several, readily accessible alternative sources, not all of which may be supportive. Not providing information can be regarded as secretive and in itself can create an issue around which a public can gather.
- The internet and mobile technologies change the power relationships between stakeholder networks because smaller interest groups can

present their case as well as large organizations and can interact directly with other stakeholders. These technologies are an activist's friend.

- Individual opinions have equal weight; no one is more important than anyone else. Opinions are formed in a different way, as traditional opinion-formers give way to new ones. In the run-up to the last US Presidential election Barack Obama invited influential bloggers to press conferences and treated them as key opinion-formers. The traditional opinion-formers, for example the offline media and community leaders, are less influential than they were.
- Communication is direct, without the mediation of, say, journalists or other traditional opinion formers. This changes not only power relationships, but also the speed and reach of communications: sometimes to groups unknown to the object of the communication.
- It is essentially a 'pull' or 'demand' medium. There are limited opportunities to 'push' information without users seeking it. Practitioners will find themselves increasingly providing demand-led information, such as responding to e-mail and website enquiries, and will need to rethink their roles in these terms.
- With their knowledge of stakeholders and their management, public relations professionals are uniquely placed to be the knowledge managers for their organizations. This new role for the public relations professional is at a higher level. They are neither technicians nor managers, but communication executives who will be regarded as the peers of the highest executives in the organization.

HOW 'RECEIVERS' USE INFORMATION

A consideration of how those who receive communication from public relation practitioners is clearly important and the process is complex. Much investigation and theorizing has been done on this topic. Many public relations practitioners want to believe in the Domino Theory[7] of the effect of communication.

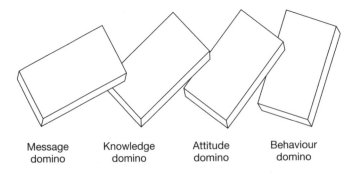

| Message domino | Knowledge domino | Attitude domino | Behaviour domino |

This is reflective of early marketing theory which was based on the AIDA model. First of all people become **A**ware of an idea or product or service but have little knowledge about it.

Then they develop an **I**nterest and seek out more information. Then they become persuaded of the benefits of the idea or product or service and develop a **D**esire to buy it. Finally they show their support by taking **A**ction and buying the product or service.

Sometimes this simple progression is achievable, but often it is not. In fact, Grunig and Hunt state that the chances of someone progressing through the dominos from the point where the message is received to behaving in a desired way are 4 in 10,000. An audience or public might learn about an organization and form a negative rather than a positive attitude, or they might develop an attitude but not take the desired action. The portrayal of wars and famines often engenders strong sympathy in the minds of television viewers and newspaper readers, but they might not make a charitable donation as a result. There is certainly no proven causal link between people thinking about something, forming an attitude and then acting in a predictable way. Public relations people may provide and present in an attractive manner all the information an individual needs to think or act in a particular way. However, the way those individuals form their attitudes and behave is usually very specific to them and their particular situation, and is not entirely predictable.

Furthermore, people are very adept at holding incompatible beliefs. For example, individuals may be vociferous supporters of measures to combat environmental pollution, but may own a car. They will therefore argue differently depending on the situation they are talking about. One thing is very clear; if someone is very firmly of a particular opinion and acts to support it, it will be very difficult to persuade him or her to a different point of view. Just giving people lots of positive information will not necessarily change their attitudes or behaviour. The leverage points have to be identified and worked upon in order to make productive shifts in awareness, attitude or behaviour. If there are no leverage points which can be worked on persuasively, the argument is lost from the start (more on this in Chapter 6).

There are other theories that provide a more sophisticated insight into how people receive information than the Domino Theory. Uses and Gratification Theory states that receivers of communication select the content that is most gratifying or useful to them. Thus, readers of an internal employee newsletter, will look at the material that most fulfils their individual social and psychological needs. Hence, if sport plays no role in their life and they find no gratification in reading about it, these items will be of no attraction.

The original formation of Uses and Gratification Theory equated 'needs' with Maslow's hierarchy, but more recent work[8] includes other kinds of gratification, including:

- information: obtaining advice, learning, orientating with different parts of the environment;
- personal identity: self-knowledge, reinforcing personal values, finding attractive models of behaviour;
- integration and social interaction: finding out about others, discovering how to relate to others, discovering how to play a role, building social interactions;
- entertainment: relaxing, escaping from problems, passing time, satisfying intellectual, physical and social needs.

Thus, receivers make a judgement about the value of the received information based on the gratification, or need-fulfilment they get from it; either immediately or for the future.

A distinction can be drawn between those people who value communication for its outcome (ie need fulfilment) and those who value it as a process (ie people enjoy the act of communication itself). Of course a mixture of the two is also quite common. However, the public relations person needs to be aware of this distinction. Some individuals and groups are satisfied with a to-the-point, 'no nonsense' communication that provides unambiguous content. Others have a need to engage in lengthy discussion or correspondence and gain gratification from that process. The implications of both cases are obvious.

While Uses and Gratification Theory is useful in identifying how receivers of communication select the content they find most useful, it does not explain how that content is interpreted, or given meaning. Reception Theory attempts to explain how people do this. The idea is that meaning is not somehow 'fixed' in the content of communication by the sender, but it needs the receiver to co-construct it on reception. Often this involves an iterative process where meanings are checked and adjusted (see also Figure 5.2), and is undertaken within the particular social and cultural environment that individuals or groups inhabit, and their own backgrounds. Thus, individuals and groups construct 'frames' or lenses through which to interpret the content of communication. They will hold these frames more or less in common with other individuals and groups and the more these frames are shared or understood, the greater the chance of a common understanding being reached. This 'cultural' understanding of what happens in the act of communication allows for the fact that content is always amenable to several interpretations and is likely to evoke different reactions; support, rejection, or a place in between. Thus, a deep knowledge of the individuals and publics that are the objects of communication is a requirement when planning public relations programmes (more on this in Chapter 6).

SETTING REALISTIC AIMS AND OBJECTIVES

Bearing all this in mind, then, we can now look at setting purposeful, stretching yet achievable aims and objectives.

First, a note on definitions; an aim is a broad statement of what the communicator wants to achieve. It does not have any specifically measurable outcomes. Objectives on the other hand are the concrete, measurable steps and activities that will help to achieve that aim. They are highly specific and, in their totality will ensure achievement of the whole aim. A simple example illustrates the difference:

Aim: maximize shareholder attendance at the next AGM

Objectives:

- identify a location for the AGM that is most accessible to shareholders 10 weeks in advance of the AGM;
- identify the best time for the meeting by sampling shareholders 10 weeks before the AGM;
- undertake a phased and integrated on- and offline communication programme in the eight-week period prior to the AGM;

and so on.

Aims

Setting the overall aim, or aims for a public relations programme, is not easy. First there has to be agreement about what the contribution of public relations will be to solving a particular issue, or capitalizing on a specific opportunity. Second, there may be different opinions about the scope of the programme and over the best way to approach the issue.

To achieve consensus on these issues, it is advisable to work collaboratively with those who are commissioning the work because they will have the biggest stake in the outcome. It must be borne in mind that the eventual programme will be judged on whether or not it has achieved its aim(s). If these are not agreed at the outset, the programme could well be judged on other criteria.

There must also be clarity over outcome and process aims. Outcome aims are those concerned with what you want publics to do: the results of the communication. Process aims are orientated around what the practitioner does to achieve the aim.'Maximize shareholder attendance at the AGM' is an outcome aim. The aim could have been stated as 'use all available mass communication techniques to maximize shareholder attendance at the AGM'. This includes a process as well as an outcome. The two are related, but should be separated.

There are some general principles to bear in mind when setting aims:

- Make them singular (one aim at a time), clear (specific) and readily understandable.
- Frame them in terms of outcomes and describe the process by which they will be achieved in overall terms if necessary.
- They should be able to be evaluated at the end of the programme by turning the aim into a question. Hence, the aim 'to improve relationships with the University's business partners' becomes the evaluative question 'did the University improve relationships with its business partners?'

It may be possible to have just one overall aim for a campaign with a relatively simple outcome, such as 'Maximize attendance by shareholders at the AGM', but if the programme is complex, multi-layered and has a number of publics or stakeholder groups involved, a number of aims will be needed, each having objectives to support their achievement. For example, in an avian flu outbreak, the aim for the general public could well be about trying to reassure them; for hospitals and doctors it will be about identification and treatment of flu victims; for those in the food industry, it will be about safety of the food chain. Of course all these aims could be subordinate to the overarching aim of ensuring the wellbeing of the nation; but the point is made, in this case the specific programme will need different aims for different publics.

Finally, aims need to be linked to organizational objectives, and targeted at societal, management or specific programme issues, or any combination of the three. That way a direct link to organizational contribution can be made.

Objectives

Objectives are the specific, measurable statements that break down the aims into the steps that must be achieved if success is to be realized. They are effectively the project milestones.

As has been stated before, public relations is purposive; communication usually has some persuasive element. The communication continuum has at one end making people aware of something, and at the other getting people to behave in particular ways with working at the attitude and opinion level being somewhere in between. There is an accepted hierarchy of objective setting then, which mirrors these three levels: awareness, attitudes and opinions, and behaviour.

- *Awareness* – getting target publics to think about something and trying to promote a level of understanding. Awareness objectives focus on information and knowledge. These are often called *cognitive* (thinking) objectives and are to do with attention, comprehension and retention.

An example could be the government wishing to make citizens aware of a change in tax rates.

- *Attitudes and opinions* – getting target publics to form a particular attitude or opinion about a subject. Attitudes are concerned with how people react to information. These are often called *affective* (feeling) objectives and are to do with interest and acceptance or rejection. An example could be a pressure group wanting moral support for changes in mental health provision.
- *Behaviour* – getting target publics to act in a desired way. These are often called *conative* (acting) objectives and are to do with promoting a desired response involving action. An example could be a local police force using local radio to ask drivers to change their route home away from a major accident site.

Bearing this in mind, there are three things that are very much in the practitioners control which helps them achieve their objectives.

- The level of objective needs to be chosen carefully. If a new or difficult idea is being introduced, the practitioners might work at the awareness levels first before moving on to the higher levels; planners should not try to obtain a behavioural response immediately unless they have legislation to back them, or their 'offer' is so powerful as to be irresistible.
- Planners can choose who the priority target publics are and, furthermore, planners can enlist the help of those individuals or groups within those target publics who are already favourably disposed towards them or who could be readily enlisted (more of this in Chapter 6).
- The persuasion doesn't need to be all one way. As stated several times, the organization can change too and sometimes relatively small changes in organizational attitude or behaviour can result in major positive effects on target public.

The principle to remember is that it is a much larger and more difficult task to get someone to act than it is to get them to think about something. So the kinds of objectives public relations programmes might have could be:

Awareness level:
- create awareness;
- promote understanding;
- inform;
- confirm a perception;
- develop knowledge.

Attitudes level:
- displace prejudice;

- encourage belief;
- overcome misunderstanding or apathy;

Behaviour level:
- act in a particular way.

GOLDEN RULES OF OBJECTIVE SETTING

There are a number of imperatives that must be borne in mind when setting objectives:

- *Ally to organizational objectives.* Public relations programmes and campaigns must support organizational objectives, otherwise effort will be dissipated on interesting but essentially trivial and tactical work. If a corporate objective is a major repositioning of the company in its market, then the public relations effort must be directed to supporting that.
- *Set public relations objectives.* Again it is a tendency of public relations professionals to set objectives that public relations cannot deliver. It is not reasonable to say that public relations should increase sales by 20 per cent if that depends on the salesforce too. It is reasonable to say that presentations should be made to 50 per cent of key retailers to tell them of new product lines and to try them. It may well be that as a result sales do increase by 20 per cent – but it is outside of the public relations practitioners' control to promise this.
- *Link to aims.* All objectives should clearly support the aims and contribute to their fulfilment.
- *Be linked to specific publics.* Vague aims around 'the general public' are just that. Be specific about the publics being worked with and what is to be to achieved.
- *Be outcome focused.* Objectives will form the basis of future evaluation so be sure to focus on outcomes, not on the process used (such as number of brochures being distributed). It is admissible to have process objectives but be clear that this is specified and differentiated from outcome objectives.
- *Research based.* Objectives should have an evidence base around them. If it is known that 60 per cent of a public act in a particular way, it may be reasonable to create an objective around increasing that to 70 per cent. However, setting a 70 per cent target based on no research is very dangerous.
- *Be singular.* Focus on the separate steps to meet the aims. Objectives with more than one element are difficult to evaluate.
- *Be precise and specific.* Objectives need to be sharp. To create awareness is not good enough. Creating awareness of what, with whom, when and how needs to be clearly spelt out.

- *Do what is achievable.* It is better to set modest objectives and hit them, than to aim for the sky and miss. Wherever possible evaluate the likely benefits of ideas and pre-test or pilot schemes. If a major part of the programme is to contact all investors to inform them of a particular development, there must be certainty that it can be done within the Stock Market rules.
- *Quantify as much as possible.* Not all objectives are precisely quantifiable, but most are. If the aim is to contact particular audience groups say how many. Quantifying objectives makes evaluation much easier. Furthermore, make sure that what is being quantifying is important and worthwhile. As Albert Einstein said, 'Not everything that counts can be counted, not everything that is counted counts'.
- *Work to a timescale.* Know when delivery is required then work can be placed or help brought in as needed. Be explicit about delivery dates.
- *Work within budget.* A good planner and manager knows exactly how much things will cost, and will design objectives with that in mind. Penetration of a particular public by 100 per cent may not be achievable within budget.
- *Work to a priority list.* Prioritizing objectives enables planners to see where the major effort is to be focused. Have enough to achieve the aim, but more than that is unnecessary and inefficient.

Remember the SMART acronym for objectives: **S**tretching, **M**easurable, **A**chievable (given other activities), **R**ealistic (having the resources to achieve them) and **T**imebound.

Examples of workable objectives are as follows:

Corporate:	Inform 10 targeted investors of reasons for management buyout before the AGM. (awareness level)
Trade:	Ensure 50 top dealers attend annual dealers' conference. (behaviour level)
Consumer:	Increase levered editorial coverage of service by 20 per cent over 18 months. (process objective, purpose is to increase sales – a behaviour-level objective)
Employees:	Maximize branch acceptance of corporate clothing by December. (90 per cent is target for acceptance) (behaviour level)
Community:	Increase support for accepting new waste recycling scheme by 10 per cent in 12 months. (attitudinal, leading in future to behavioural level)

CONSTRAINTS ON AIMS AND OBJECTIVES

Of course it would be nice to plan without any form of constraint, but there are usually a number of factors that have to be given careful regard. These are either internally or externally generated.

Internal constraints

- *Who should do the job?* The capabilities of the people assigned to the task need careful assessment. Are they able to carry it out? If not, will this mean that the demands of the task will have to be limited? Alternatively, is it possible to enlist the help of other people such as a public relations consultancy? Are there enough people for the task? Again can extra hands be drafted in or will the scope of the task need to be reduced?
- *How much will it cost?* No one has an open-ended budget so what are the effects on a prioritized programme of any budgetary constraints? What can be left out if necessary or for what should a case for additional resources be made?
- *When does it need to happen?* Sometimes an internal timetable will require that the public relations task has to be carried out at a certain time, for example, the announcement of a major company restructure or the introduction of a new process.
- *Who makes the decisions?* Are the public relations professionals able to decide on the appropriate courses of action or is the power elsewhere, such as with a marketing director?
- *Is the support in place?* Is there the right administrative back-up and physical resources such as IT support and video production, to support the programme?

External constraints

- *Who is the programme trying to reach?* What is the range of publics or audiences? How many are there? What is their geographical spread? What are their preferred media? What about their socio-economic grouping?
- *What are the socio-cultural differences?* What are the different media conventions in the various countries being operating in? What social and cultural differences and protocols have to be observed?
- *What infrastructure support is there?* What facilities such as mobile phone network coverage or access to computers are available?
- *Time frames?* Are there certain calendar dates such as New Year or a national holidays that have to be met? What about other key events such as the Grand Prix or the Ideal Home Exhibition?

DIFFERENT LEVELS OF AIMS AND OBJECTIVES

Aims and objectives can, of course, apply to whole programmes or individual projects. They can also operate at various levels: societal, corporate and programme.

The example below shows how issues that an organization faces translate into aims and objectives at the various levels.

ISSUE	AIM	OBJECTIVE
Company seen as old-fashioned (management)	Position as company that is innovative	Promote product as an exemplar of innovation
Company not seen as contributor to local communities (societal)	Position as company that takes public responsibility seriously	Promote company-sponsored recycling scheme in community
Company to contribute to be seen as caring employer (programme: employees)	Demonstrate company's ongoing commitment to employees	Promote well-being scheme

The setting of good, realistic aims and objectives is fundamental to the success of public relations plans. They provide the whole basis of the programme by clearly setting down what the key achievements must be. They become the rationale behind the strategy, set the agenda for the actions to be taken and provide the benchmark for evaluation further down the road. When put into practice, they also guide management decisions, such as where to cut resources if necessary, or where to expand the budget and put in extra effort.

The temptation to over-promise must be resisted. That is not so say that public relations practitioners should set themselves soft targets; they should be as rigorous as any other business area and based on careful research. They must, however, recognize the complexity of the communication process, and be realistic about what shifts in attitude and behaviour can be achieved.

Programmes that aim to produce radical shifts in attitude and behaviour usually take a great deal of time and are bound initially to meet with a limited amount of success. There are, of course, exceptions that break the rule, and these are often triggered by a crisis or the creation of a 'hot issue' that is fuelled by the media. Generally speaking, however, the most success-ful programmes start from the point of where the publics are, and attempt to make incremental shifts which, over a period of time, can be seen to have made considerable progress. The reputations of the best companies have taken considerable time to build. Public relations activity is to do with building reputations, too, and that is a slow and painstaking business.

Notes

1. Shannon, C and Weaver, W (1949) *The Mathematical Theory of Communi-cation*, Universty of Illinois Press, Urbana, IL.
2. Schramm, W (1954) How communication works, in *The Process and Effects of Mass Communication*, ed W Schramm, University of Illinois Press, Urbana, IL.
3. Rogers, E M and Kincaid, D L (1981) *Communication Networks: Towards a New Paradigm for Research*, The Free Press, New York.
4. First proposed by J M McLeod and S H Chaffee (1977) in Interpersonal approaches to communication research, *American Behavioural Scientist*, **16**, pp 469–500, but since then refined and applied specifically to public relations.
5. First proposed by E Katz and P F Lazarsfeld in *Personal Influence,* Free Press, Glencoe.
6. See Windahl, S, Signitzer, B with Olson, J (2009) *Using Communication Theory*, Sage, London, for further explanation.
7. Grunig, J E and Hunt, T (1984) *Managing Public Relations*, Holt, Rinehart and Winston, New York.
8. See Windahl, S, Signitzer, B with Olson, J (2009) *Using Communication Theory*, Sage, London, for further explanation.

6

Knowing the publics and messages

WHO SHALL WE TALK TO AND WHAT SHALL WE SAY?

Having answered the question 'Where am I going?' by setting achievable aims and objectives, the next question to ask is 'Who shall I talk to?'

By undertaking formative research for the proposed programme an analysis of the attitudes of each of the stakeholders and publics that relate to the organization will be available. Now the closer stakeholders, referred to as publics because of the organization's specific relationship with them around specific issues, need to have a priority order put on them and a decision on how to interact with them. Sometimes the priorities are fairly obvious. If there is to be a launch of a new product, the primary audiences are going to be existing and potential customers. However, sometimes dialogue needs to be started with groupings with whom the organization has had little or nothing to do. If the organization is a private company seeking a stock market listing for the first time, then it will need to speak to the City, specialist financial journalists and opinion-formers in the sector who influence potential investors, and will have to begin from scratch.

There are groupings of publics that are fairly common to most organizations. These are shown in Figure 6.1.

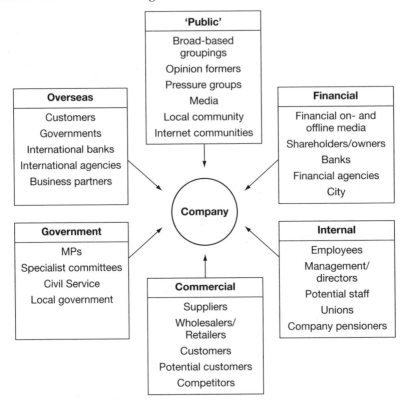

Figure 6.1 *Publics common to most organizations*

Again it is a common failing of public relations practitioners that they perform a rather simple and crude chopping up of the publics that organizations have. They believe that a particular grouping contains individuals who all act in the same way.

In Chapter 5, where objective setting was discussed, it was shown that radical shifts in attitude and behaviour are very difficult to achieve. It is vital therefore that there is understanding of what can be achieved with particular audiences or publics and the different sub-groupings within them.

WHAT IS PUBLIC OPINION?

It is worth spending a little time discussing public opinion since what practitioners are trying to do in public relations is shift the balance of opinion of the various publics interacted with in favour of their organization. It has already been noted that understanding the broader context that those publics inhabit is essential. Public opinion can be broadly regarded as the prevalent view held by the majority of people. It is against this background that work with particular publics takes place. One definition of public opinion is as follows:

> Public opinion represents a consensus, which emerges over time, from all the expressed views that cluster around an issue in debate, and that this consensus exercises power.[1]

Public opinion works two ways: it is both a cause and effect of public relations activity. Public opinion, strongly held, affects management decisions. For example, increasing concerns for the environment has affected the motor and furniture industries. Noxious emissions from cars have been cut and trade in non-replantable hardwoods is frowned on. Public relations practitioners ensure management are aware of public opinion so that they can make decisions in the light of it. Practitioners also publicize the fact that their organizations care for the environment and thereby attempt to gain public support for their organization.

On the other hand, a stated objective of many public relations programmes is to affect the general public and often this means or implies affecting public opinion, often by mounting a media relations campaign. The commonly held view is that public opinion is 'what is in the media' and if what the media says can be affected, public opinion will also change because the media help to set the public agenda.

Most people have opinions on most things, they only have to be asked. These opinion may be strongly or weakly held. The fear of many public relations practitioners is that these opinions could be drawn together and focused by the media against their organization. The hope is by getting an organization's message out, mass opinion will be supportive. Thus many public relations programmes adopt a scattergun approach, spreading very general messages via mass communication channels to very broad publics.

Research in the United States[2] has found that only 21 per cent of Americans aged between 18 and 24 and 37 per cent of those aged between 35 and 49 read newspapers regularly. (This increased to 56 per cent for those over 65.) Web-based news consumption among these groups was 7 per cent, 11 per cent and 3 per cent respectively.

This apparent lack of interest has a complex explanation. Generally speaking, news consumption is fragmenting as people use a plethora of sources to obtain news, but according to the Pew Research Center news consumption overall is declining as other forms of entertainment become more readily available. In addition, most people have neither the time nor the energy to be involved in everything. They are selective and devote time to those things that they are involved in, and where they feel they can make a contribution.

Uniform public opinion occurs very occasionally and well-informed public opinion occurs even more rarely. What uniformity there is is increasingly under threat as people turn to many different sources of news, each with very different editorial sources and some with no pretence of being objective.

Having said this, the media still play a role in setting the public mood and agenda and, interestingly, the mainstream media are often the primary sources of information for online opinion formers, so their influence is still extensive.

The media do not determine what people think; but they do provide a platform for discussing issues and they can reinforce the 'public' view if a particular issue catches the imagination.

However, what appears to be a small proportion of the total population (for example students) concerned with a particular issue (developing world indebtedness) can be a large group when all banded together and can affect the mission of a large organization (eg the banks).

Opinions are very interesting phenomena and can operate at different levels. Asked for a view of something in the news, most people will offer an opinion. That might be superficial and not always thought-through. These views might be called perceptions. At a deeper level people may have an opinion about a particular issue such as hanging, which has been well thought-through and for which they can produce arguments. They can be said to have a particular attitude towards that subject. At an even deeper level attitudes can turn into forms of behaviour. At the most extreme, this could take the form of direct action which could be against the law, such as some of the activities of the more militant animal rights groups.

To make things even more complicated, as indicated earlier, people can hold two conflicting opinions at the same time. For example, they might think animal experiments are wrong in general, but also believe that certain types of drugs should be tested on animals before being used on human beings.

TYPES OF PUBLICS

In general terms, publics can be divided into active or passive. James Grunig[3] defines four sorts of publics:

- *Non-publics*, which are groups that neither are affected by nor affect the organization. For example, a retailer based in southern India will have no effect on and will not be affected by publics based in northern India. Broadly speaking, these publics can be ignored and are often not even identified.
- *Latent publics*, which are groups that face a problem as a result of an organization's actions, but fail to recognize it. For example, a haulage company expanding its business may increase local traffic levels, yet the local residents may be unaware of this.
- *Aware publics*, which are groups that recognize that a problem exists. In our haulage company example, the local residents may read a press story that tells them about the expansion.
- *Active publics*, which are groups that do something about the problem. For example, local residents may blockade the haulage company's gates.

Active publics can be further broken down into three categories:

- *All-issue publics* are active on all issues affecting an organization. For instance, that public might be opposed to the organization in principle and try to disrupt all its activities. An example of this is the anti-nuclear lobby, which will oppose all the work of any company involved in handling nuclear material, even that which may be non-nuclear-related.
- *Single-issue publics* are active on one issue or a small set of issues – for example, the Save the Whale campaign. They might not be opposed to an organization per se, but will oppose any activity that is contrary to their view on that particular issue. In fact publics may be broadly supportive of an organization, but totally opposed to one particular activity, such as giving advantageous share options to directors.
- *Hot-issue publics* are those involved in an issue that has broad public support and usually gets extensive media coverage. An example of this would be the public support for Greenpeace over the issue of the disposal of the Brent Spar oil platform.

There are also what Grunig calls:

- *Apathetic publics*, which are publics basically unconcerned by all problems and are effectively not a public at all. However, some theorists would argue that these publics are a grouping that should concern public relations practitioners – everyone has the potential to become interested in an issue.

When an organization or its publics behave in such a way that the other is affected, then a problem or issue arises. Publics, Grunig argues, are created by specific situations and the problems or opportunities they cause. There is no such thing as a 'general' situation or a 'general' public.

Responses to issues depend very much on individual circumstances. Why is it, with the best of intentions, people sometimes just don't get round to writing that cheque for that good cause?

Grunig provides some explanations about when and how people communicate and when communications aimed at particular publics are likely to be effective. He says that there are three main factors that need to be taken into account:

- *Problem recognition* – In essence, people won't think about a situation unless they believe that something needs to be done about it, ie they have a problem. If there is a group of people who are actively seeking information about a situation, they are more likely to become 'aware' or 'active' publics than those who just passively receive the information without making any effort. So the communications professional will need to identify those 'information seekers', provide them with what they need and enter into a dialogue; otherwise, they may go elsewhere and obtain less than supportive material. In the example of the haulage company that is expanding, the public relations professional would need to identify those people who perceive the company's expansion plans as problematic, find out those who want information and provide an appropriate channel of communication; otherwise, they might contact an anti-traffic lobby for advice and information.

  Those people who recognize that they have a problem often seek information as a precursor to action; so the provision of information is vital.

- *Constraint recognition* – This is the extent to which people perceive that there are constraints on their ability to act in the way they want. So if people think there is little or nothing they can do about the expansion of a haulage company, they will probably want none or limited practical information about its operations. If, however, they believe that they can do something, they will communicate with all kinds of organizations to get information and advice.

While problem recognition and constraint recognition often determine what information a public will want about a situation, the third factor usually affects their behaviour.

- *Level of involvement* – This is how connected someone feels to a situation. So if people live next door to the haulage company, they may feel very involved because they are likely to be most affected by the increase in traffic. Those four streets away may not be as affected, so may not become actively involved, even if they recognize the problem and think they could do something about it.

So from the public relations professional's point of view, those people who are highly involved in an issue usually have strong problem recognition and minimal constraints. They are likely to be most active and to demand most information. Those not involved or who face high levels of constraints may be aware publics, but are unlikely to become active unless they become involved or their constraints are removed. Their situation needs to be monitored so as to avoid any surprise when they do become active.

The approach of Grunig allows us to define publics for organizations from two angles:

- First of all, a public is defined by considering very carefully exactly who will be affected by the policies and activities of that organization.
- Second, by monitoring the environment it is possible to identify those publics that have particular interests in specific issues, whose opinion and behaviour will significantly affect the activities of the organization.

This apparently theoretical approach is useful, since if an organization identifies its issues-based publics it will pinpoint those who are likely to be the activists on any particular issue. This is particularly important when dealing with internet communities, which we have seen (Chapter 5) form around issues.

From this it is clear that active publics are the most likely to use information from public relations programmes as a prompt for their behaviour. They will only be a proportion of the targeted population; however, it is important to identify them since communication effort should be focused on them.

A further note of caution is needed. Grunig says that if attitudes or behaviour objectives are changed (remembering that you will probably have raised awareness already), don't expect to affect more than 20 per cent of the target group and don't forget that some of these will be negative in their response. The importance of researching the attitudes of the various publics, what they think of the organization and how they act so that organizations can understand and communicate more effectively, cannot be overemphasized.

It is, of course, eminently sensible to put together the traditional way of segmenting publics into consumers, employees, etc, with Grunig's approach. The broader categories can be analysed for those subgroups that are likely to be active, aware and latent. It brings a very potent communication perspective and helps prioritize the actions of the communicator.

Grunig's work has been criticized as not being sensitive to cultural or diversity issues, that it does not properly engage with the differences in power between the communicating partners or the fact that people have relationships with organizations at many levels and in many different types of situation. Nonetheless, it does promote a good starting point for considering publics and the fact that publics collect around issues is a seminal insight.

USING OTHER SEGMENTATION TECHNIQUES

Apart from Grunig's method of identifying publics there are others that are used by public relations practitioners. A common method is to use 'segmentation' techniques. There are several ways publics can be segmented or categorized and the best way will be determined by the nature of the programme. For example, a government wanting to promote responsible driving may segment by age, gender and type of car. A youth club wanting new members may segment by age and proximity to the club. An online clothing retailer will segment by age, income, lifestyle and gender. There are many ways to segment publics:

- by geography – where they live, work, go on holiday;
- by demographics – age, gender, income, social class;
- by psychographics – attitudes, opinions, beliefs;
- by group membership – of clubs, societies, professional associations;
- by media consumption – of newspapers, magazines, websites;
- by type of power:
  - overt: religious leader, opinion former
  - covert: influence, connectedness;
- by role in decision process – financial director, CEO, parent, head teacher.

A common practice is to identify the two most important variables for the situation being addressed and to create a matrix with these two variables as axes to segment publics.

One of the most popular is the power/interest matrix used by strategic business planners.[4]

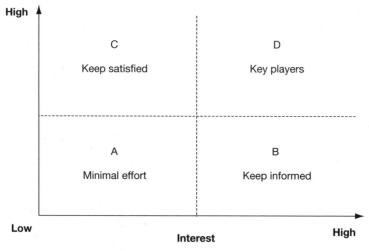

Figure 6.2 *Power/interest matrix*

The author has seen other variables such as credibility and reach, resources and influence used in a similar way.

The power/interest matrix categorizes publics according to the amount of power they have (and that needs to be defined; is it resource power, influence over others, power by virtue of their role, political power etc?) and the level of interest they have in the issue that is the focus of the public relations programme (and interest needs to be defined: is it personal interest, do they represent others and is the interest positive or negative, etc?). The more power and interest they have, the more likely they will impact on the organization: hence their label – key players have most power and most interest.

It is possible and desirable at times to move publics from one segment to another. For example, shareholders often reside in segment C, their interest being limited if the company is performing well. However, in times of crisis, it might be desirable to stimulate their interest so that they become positive and active supporters of the company, in which case increased communication will be used to move them to segment D. Similarly, activist groups can often be placed in segment B; they have a lot of interest. By keeping them informed and addressing their issues as far as possible, it may be possible to move them towards segment A, or at least prevent them from seeking means to achieve power and hence becoming key players.

When applying this model to the public and third sectors, care is needed. Groups without power or interest are usually given minimal attention in the private sector: they are regarded as unimportant. However, in the public or third sectors it can be the reverse. Many charities exist to give a voice to those who have little power or have no interest in issues that might affect them. In the public sector, hard to reach groups who have little power and whose interest is blocked by practical issues such as an inability to read or to speak the dominant language, can be found in this segment.

By carefully plotting publics in the grid it is possible to identify who the potential advocates or opponents are and how communication should be used to engage with them. For example, more information may empower a group. By focusing on issues that concern them specifically, it will be possible to stimulate their interest. A visual tool such as this helps to identify more easily who should be repositioned on the grid and where they are relative to other players. By exploring scenarios it will help to show how stakeholders may move as the scenario develops. Their potential movement may or may not be desirable and preventative action can then be considered.

In social marketing campaigns, which are designed to stimulate behavioural change about some of the larger issues that affect society as a whole, a detailed examination of target publics is undertaken in order to gain Insight: a technical term meaning a profound understanding of people that is then used to identify the mechanisms that will change their behaviour. This is a three-stage process involving data collection (the what), obtaining key understandings (the why) in order to identify the key levers that will generate behaviour change (the how).

Data collection comes from four sources: an environmental analysis (outlined as EPISTLE in Chapter 2), existing studies (for example from databases), commissioned research (for example, through a questionnaire) and then an in-depth understanding of the publics whose behaviour you want to change (obtained, for example, from observation).

In addition to this, a detailed understanding of who exactly the target publics are (demographics), their attitudes and opinions (psychographics) and what they do (behaviours), will provide a rich picture.

Drawing all this information together, analysing it and synthesizing it then leads to some fundamental understandings of the issue, how people associate with it and, specifically, how they can be motivated to change – this last part is the resultant Insight.

Insight is vital in behaviour-change programmes. It helps to develop that 'killer' proposition that makes people want to change their behaviour. For example, in the early 2000s there was a problem with young people, in particular, not wanting to use rear seat belts. They felt rear seat belts were restrictive and uncomfortable, wearing them indicated distrust of the driver, seat belts were for little kids and rear passengers were not as vulnerable as those in the front. Research also revealed that many drivers were killed by unbelted rear seat passengers, who smashed into them from the back of the car.

The insight arrived at from the research and a deep understanding of the target publics was that they certainly did not want to be responsible for the deaths of drivers, people who they often knew and loved. A campaign built around this insight increased seat belt use by that group by 23 per cent over just one year.

SO WHAT ABOUT THE MEDIA?

Earlier the role of the media in influencing public opinion was played down, but it is obvious that it does have a powerful impact in our lives. Here are some general observations.

The media are more likely to create a public when the information is negative. People react against child abuse or government officials being overpaid as they see it. If the coverage is extensive and the topic catches the imagination it is possible that a hot-issue public could be created.

Hot-issue publics often react to the thing of the moment without necessarily thinking things through carefully, and once media interest dies down, so does theirs. However, if an organization handles a hot issue badly it could turn hot-issue publics into longer-term active ones by forcing them to think more deeply about the issues concerned. The growing support for 'natural foods' is a case in point.

Media campaigns to promote organizations are most likely to reach active publics who positively seek out any information about the organization they are interested in. This includes those who are opposed to them as well as those who may support them. Thinking through the consequences and likely reactions of those who feel negatively about the organization when seeking media coverage is, therefore, very important.

THE IMPLICATIONS FOR TARGETING PUBLICS

The implications of all this are fairly obvious. Don't devote too much time on publics that are not interested in what is being done or said, but always keep an eye on them just in case. Of course, if the aim is to reach a disinterested public, practitioners will have to be creative about how they reach them and it will usually take more time and effort to accomplish objectives. There will be a need to research what issues there are that are important to them and to attach to those interest points. Active publics are the 'communicators' friend'. They positively seek out and want to understand information. On the downside it is possible to keep a low profile with them, however, if they are not supplied with information, they will seek it from elsewhere and being active it could be that they will act against the organization as well as for it.

Don't expect changes in attitude and behaviour from huge numbers of publics or for it to happen quickly. Only a proportion of active and aware publics are likely to respond. However, they can act as catalysts for change and their power should not be underestimated.

HOW TO PRIORITIZE PUBLICS

If initiating or rebuilding a public relations department from scratch the practitioner will need to make an assessment about which publics are most important and how much time should be devoted to them.

The easiest way to categorize publics is to move from the general to the particular. First of all define broad categories to identify their connections with the organization. Divide these broad categories into particular groups. This could be done on the basis of geography or the level of activity likely from the group, or on the power and influence of that group.

Prioritize the groups. An example is given in Table 6.1 (the groupings are very broad, but the principle holds). For individual programmes or campaigns the same principles can be applied, although the headings will

Table 6.1 *Proportioning out the public relations effort to different publics*

Grouping	Percentage of communication effort required	
Corporate		25
Shareholders (active)	10	
Shareholders (latent)	2	
Government ministers (active)	4	
Government ministers (aware)	3	
Opposition front bench (active)	3	
Opposition front bench (aware)	1	
Senior civil servants	2	
Customers		25
ABC1 householders (current purchasers)	10	
ABC1 householders (potential)	5	
Retail shops (active)	7	
Retail shops (new)	3	
Employees		20
Executives	3	
Supervisors	7	
Shopfloor workers	7	
Trade union leaders	3	
Community		15
Neighbours	4	
Community leaders	5	
Schools		
Headteachers	2	
PTA	2	
Governors	2	
Suppliers		9
Raw materials		
major suppliers	6	
minor suppliers	3	
Services		6
major suppliers	4	
minor suppliers	2	

be different depending on various publics are segmented. The amount of effort and time that is required for each public will be determined by any confirmation of factors specific to the situation, including importance, urgency, power, legitimacy and how communicative the organization wishes to be.

The overall level of activity is likely to be limited by budget.

Remember that individuals or groups can belong to more than one category so there needs to be identification and monitoring of the crossovers to ensure that publics are treated equitably, and so that conflicting content is not available, even if there are differences in emphasis or different content depending on the needs of different publics: co-ordination is vital.

WHAT SHALL WE SAY?

Devising the content of a programme or campaign is a complex business and very specific to the individual situation. There are a number of considerations that need to be taken into account. First, the nature of the programme itself.

The nature of the programme

There are three main types of programmes or campaigns.

Information campaigns: seek to transmit information and do not encourage dialogue. They are essentially one way. It is perfectly legitimate to conduct an information campaign. For example, a doctor's surgery may wish to inform patients about extended opening hours. In essence this is a transmission of factual information. Clarity and the use of appropriate channels are the key elements for success here.

Persuasion campaigns: seek to persuade people to a particular view, ie to affect their attitudes or to influence their behaviour in some way. Social marketing campaigns fall into this category. The originating organization presents a case as persuasively as possible, in order to evoke a specific response. Use of appropriate channels is obviously required and a level of dialogue is to be anticipated as arguments develop.

Persuasive campaigns are often the purpose of public relations activity, and some of the descriptors the industry uses, for example, lobbying or advocacy, underline that. Persuasive campaigns cover the whole gamut of public relations activity, from consumer campaigns promoting products, to election campaigns, to government campaigns wanting to promote certain behaviours such as online submission of tax returns, to activist groups promoting their particular cause.

Dialogue-based campaigns: in these types of campaign organizations and groups communicate as peers, the one learning from the other, seeking mutual benefits and sharing on an equal basis. Dialogue can promote understanding, joint decision making and action, and deepens relationships, reputations and respect. Well-conducted dialogue is essential for relationships of trust to develop.

It must be borne in mind, however, that not all dialogue results in the positive. Sometimes, dialogue reveals deep differences and divisions, but if this occurs, dialogue can help to promote an understanding and hopefully a respect for the other point of view, even if the end result is an agreement not to agree. Hence, dialogue can have a twin purpose: to build coalitions where there is consensus, and/or to identify areas of potential conflict and then work towards a resolution of the issues involved.

Clearly dialogue requires open and two-way channels of communication. The content will be emerging, developing and multi-layered as people strive to make sense using the frames alluded to earlier in the book. Dialogue could well involve persuasion as each party makes their case, sometimes forcefully, but it will also involve information and a willingness to be persuaded.

'Deliberative engagement' is a phrase used to describe dialogue-based campaigns that result in decision making by the target public, which are then taken up by the organization initiating the dialogue. It is a technique being used increasingly by the public sector in the UK. An example of how this works can be found at www.koganpage.com/PlanningAndManaging PublicRelationsCampaigns.com if you take a look at the Norfolk case study.

CONSTRUCTING THE CONTENT

Having decided what the nature of the interaction will be, the content then has to be developed accordingly. It is generally accepted that communication is made up of both rational and emotional content.

Rational content

The use of rational arguments to persuade goes back to Greek times. The rhetoricians used logic and reason to invest their arguments with power. Smith[5] has put together a summary of the main arguments contained in the research on persuasive communication and concludes the following: the primary idea behind a persuasive speech, advertisement, e-letter or other communication vehicle is called a proposition.

There are four kinds of proposition:

- *Fact:* based on what actually exists or is the case and is provable. Facts are often used to enhance awareness or understanding.

- *Conjecture:* based on what it is reasonable to conclude given the evidence and inviting the identified public to agree. Conjecture is used to gain acceptance and/or support.
- *Value:* these types of proposition focus on the virtue or intrinsic worth of something. This aims to increase interest or build positive opinions. For example, the merits of giving asylum to a persecuted minority may be argued on virtue grounds.
- *Policy:* argues for the adoption of a new policy, and is aimed at forming opinions and affecting behaviour. For example, advocating an increase in the school-leaving age.

Propositions are backed by strong arguments and proof wherever possible. Where action is required they are also accompanied by the removal of any barriers. Smith goes on to say that physical evidence to support propositions is the most compelling, but in many situations that is just not available. There are other types of 'evidence' that can be used where it is impossible to provide physical evidence. For example:

- *Analogies:* using familiar situations and illustrations to draw parallels so that understanding is facilitated. Analogies are often presented as similes or metaphors. So, for example, twittering can be likened to gossiping, only on the internet.
- *Comparisons:* by identifying a particular characteristic or value relating to an issue and then making positive or negative association with something familiar. Comparing political parties' records on education with one another will put one or the other in a better light.
- *Examples:* the public is able to draw conclusions because of examples that are relevant. For example, you know this product is reliable, because the other six in the range have all been so.
- *Statistics:* to provide reliable evidence that claims are true. For example, this is a good school because we have statistics to prove excellent pupil performance over 10 years.
- *Testimonials and endorsements:* testimonials are provided by people who have used services and products. Endorsements are provided by people who are prepared to back the cause or the ideas of the organization. For example, testimonials about services provided by a firm of accountants are a common feature of their publicity material. Endorsements are often sought from celebrities, for example celebrities supporting fundraising efforts on telethons.
- *Case studies:* detailed examples provided by users of services or products, or of causes that have been supported that encourage adoption by others.
- *Visual evidence:* such as photographs, charts, blogs, online videos, animated websites, diagrams, illustrations and so on all add power to content.

- *Demonstrations, presentations, exhibitions:* often provide a way to present first-hand experiences of products or services.

Emotional content

Human beings can sometimes respond to rational arguments alone. However, most human beings require a mixture of both rational and emotional content to evoke a reaction. The public relations planner will have to make a judgement on the correct mix of rational and emotional appeal that they need to put into the campaign. It is likely that campaigns about returning tax forms promptly will be more rational in nature, whereas campaigns about engagement rings will be more emotional.

On occasion there are deliberate cross-overs from what might be regarded as more naturally rational campaigns, to draw people in emotionally and so encourage sales. For example, toilet rolls are a commodity product, but Andrex have used their puppy Labrador for years to create an emotional attachment to the product via a cute and vulnerable dog.

Emotions are used either positively or negatively. Smith provides four examples of positive emotional appeals:

Love appeals: these focus on the many aspects of love – family, pity, compassion, sympathy, bittersweet, etc. Love-based images are very powerful and are often used by charities for fundraising.

Virtue appeals: these can be used rationally, but they can also be used emotionally. Linking campaigns to the community and individual sense of what is right and proper is very powerful. Hence, calls to enlist during wartime, for organ donation and volunteering all draw on appeals to virtue.

Humour appeals: good for reinforcing existing attitudes and behaviours, but not very effective in changing them. Humour makes the originator more liked, but rarely more credible. Humour should be used to complement a message, not as a substitute. It also needs to be tasteful and genuinely funny.

Sex appeal: a difficult area. Sex appeal can range from the suggestive to the outrageous. Sex appeal content can demand attention, but great care has to be used to ensure it is appropriate to the target group and that it is not offensive. An issue with sex appeal is that often the sexual content is remembered, but not the brand. Footballer David Beckham has famously modelled underpants, but less people remember that the brand was Armani. The most effective way to use sexual content is if there is a strong link to the product or theme, for example links to contraceptive devices or underage sexual activity.

Smith also provides two examples of content based on negative emotion:

Fear appeals: these aim to affect behaviour directly. Fear appeals must be accompanied by an easy and immediate solution to the problem. The key to effective fear appeals is that they must be proportionate. Put too strongly and people can avoid the issue or defy it. Also, without a ready solution, no matter how great the fear is, people will feel powerless and remain inactive. Source credibility is critical in fear appeals, and the source is best when it is quite dissimilar to the target public. Hence, use of scientists, unknown to the public, is a common ploy. Obviously, if the issue is important or significant to the target public, it will also have more effect. The thought of a large refuse tip being located within smelling distance of their houses is likely to galvanize community action.

Guilt appeals: aim at promoting a sense of personal guilt or shame. As with fear appeals, guilt should be used in moderation and providing a route from feeling guilty towards a more positive frame of mind, such as feeling fair or just, is the mirror of offering a solution in fear appeals. For example, people may feel guilty about poverty in Africa, but also want to feel they can help to solve that by being generous and fair.

One final thought: as Smith points out, when conducting fear or guilt campaigns, careful consideration must be given to any ethical implications.

Content and messages

Earlier in this chapter information and persuasion campaigns were discussed and it was argued that there are right and proper uses for these types of campaign. Often campaigns of this type have messages that the originator wants to get across. Even in dialogue-based communication there may again be some core content, which may be described as messages, that each party will want to register as important, or even as non-negotiable.

The new kind of engagement with publics mainly assisted by new technologies is driving public relations towards being dialogue-based; however, the notion of core content or messages does have relevance, but requires careful thought.

Messages have utility for two additional reasons. First of all they are an essential part of the awareness and attitude-forming process. If publics play back to the originator the message that the originator has initiated, it is a clear indication (a) that the message has been received and (b) that the message has been taken on board and is in some way being used. That may be just as a part of the thinking process, or it may permeate as far as actions.

The second reason is that they help to demonstrate the effectiveness of the communication. They are an essential part of the evaluation process. If distinct messages are utilized directly by the press, or if they are repeated in evaluative research such as attitude surveys, that clearly shows the messages have been assimilated.

Content and the messages within it are often under-crafted, but they are vitally important. They are the point of contact between an organization and its publics in communication terms. They are what are 'given' by the organization and 'received' by the public and vice versa. Messages and the way they are conveyed are the starting point of the thinking, attitude or behavioural change that the organization is seeking. Badly done, they can be the end point too.

CRAFTING MESSAGES

There are four steps in crafting persuasive messages:

- *Step one* is to take existing articulated perceptions. For example, it may be that an organization's products are regarded as old-fashioned and this has been identified in earlier research.
- *Step two* is to define what shifts can be made in those perceptions. If, in fact, the products have been substantially upgraded this needs to be said loud and clear.
- *Step three* is to identify elements of persuasion. The best way to do this, as indicated earlier, is to work on the basis of fact. The organization might be making major investments in upgrading their plant. It could be that there has been a series of new technology initiatives. Maybe they have won an innovation award recently. These are all facts that falsify the view that their products are old-fashioned.
- *Step four* is to ensure how the messages can be credibly delivered through public relations.

Messages can be general in nature. Sometimes they have an overall corporate thrust. Advertising pay-off lines or company straplines such as Peugeot's 'The lion goes from strength to strength' are a good example. The organization's message is that it is healthy, growing and successful.

These general messages are often backed up by very specific sub-messages which may pinpoint a particular piece of information or a specific service that an organization wants to put across.

For example, the Royal Mail has a main message on its commitment to the local community.

It also has various sub-messages to illustrate the main message 'Royal Mail cares about the community'. Among them are, 'Royal Mail makes charitable donations', 'Royal Mail is a sponsor of events, organizations, people and/or initiatives which contribute positively to the community' and Royal Mail 'is an ethical and responsible company'.

Again, as mentioned earlier, it is important that messages do not conflict as people can belong to more than one public. It is perfectly feasible for there to be differences in nuance, or for messages to differ from one public to another, but the overall thrust of the messages must be in broad sympathy with each other.

HOW THE MESSAGE SHOULD BE PRESENTED

The integrity of a message is affected by a whole host of things that determine whether it is taken seriously or not:

- *Format.* How is the message put across? Are there visual images that are associated with it? The care taken with the physical presentation of a corporate identity is a good example of this. The appropriate words, even typeface, must be used to get across the impact of the message. Bold, joking messages often use brash, elaborate typefaces, serious material uses serif typefaces. A financial institute is probably not going to use funny cartoons to put across a death benefit product.
- *Tone.* Choice of language is very important. All messages need to have careful attention paid to the mood, atmosphere or style that they are trying to portray. The mood might be upbeat or sombre. This point is carefully linked to the format issue.
- *Context.* The context in which a message is seen is vital. If, for example, an organization announces its company results on the day a stock market slide occurs, its performance will be commented on in the light of this.
- *Timing.* It is no use pumping out information about the special Christmas offers if Christmas was last week.
- *Repetition.* Obviously the more often a credible message is repeated, the more likely it is to be heard and picked up. However, familiarity can breed contempt and care has to be taken not to repeat messages for the sake of it or they will become devalued. Using a raft of communication channels can help, since in the mind of the receiver there can be a reinforcement of credibility if they see the message in different contexts and endorsed by different media and other third parties.

On top of these points there are three things that need to be said about the source from which content or messages emanate:

- *Credibility:* the source of the message or content should be credible, that is they must be believable. A credible source is one that is seen to have the right to speak because they have the expertise or knowledge, are of the right status and are seen to be a person of honesty and integrity.
- *Personability:* the source needs to be seen to be sympathetic or empathetic to the issue. It also helps if the public sees them as a person they can relate to.
- *Control:* a source may need to be able to demonstrate a measure of control over the situation in hand. Some sources do have power and authority. For example, at the end of the day a government can legislate to change behaviour and/or punish those who do not conform. The ability to stand up to, or for something and not be found wanting is a key element to reputation and relationship building.

Having command over all these factors is likely to be a tall order: a meticulously planned media event can be ruined bcause of a breaking news story, more positively there are always opportunities that suddenly occur which can be taken advantage of even if the context is not the best possible.

Sometimes the choice of media in which content is relayed is restricted and not seen to be ideal. An annual report is a legal document and some of the information in it is strictly regulated. At other times the message imperative will dictate the communication channel. A product recall dictates that advertising and the internet will be used to get the message out as quickly and in as controlled a format as possible, despite the fact that the world will know of about the problems, even those who haven't purchased the product.

It is often the case that content and messages are not given the meticulous attention they deserve in public relations programmes. General messages are all very well in themselves, but particular publics should be served by carefully researched and constructed messages set within the proper context and medium if the communication is to do a specific job of work. Vague content in communication brings about vague results. Carefully researched, sharply refined and aimed content and messages may have an opportunity to deliver the desired effects.

Notes

1. Cutlip, S M, Center, A H and Broom, G M (2006) *Effective Public Relations*, Prentice-Hall, Upper Saddle River, NJ, 9th edn.
2. Pew Research Center, Biennial News Consumption Survey, 2008.
3. Grunig, J E and Hunt, T (1984) *Managing Public Relations*, Holt, Rinehart & Winston, New York.
4. Johnson, J, Scholes, K and Whittington, R (2007) *Exploring Corporate Strategy*, Pearson Education, London, 8th edn.
5. Smith, R D (2009) *Strategic Planning for Public Relations*, Lawrence Erlbaum Associates, Mahwah, NJ, 3rd edn.

7

Strategy and tactics

The fifth basic question in the planning process asked in Chapter 3 was 'How shall I say it?' – what mechanisms shall be used to communicate? The answer to this question falls into two parts: strategy and tactics.

GETTING THE STRATEGY RIGHT

Moving immediately from objectives or content to tactics is a temptation planners should resist. Devising the strategy for a plan or campaign is the most difficult part of the planning process. If the strategy is right, everything else rolls off the back of it.

Rather than thinking of a cohesive and coherent strategy, many practitioners move straight to tactics, the 'What shall we do?' part of the programme, rather than considering carefully about how the overall programme should be shaped. They then end up with a fragmented, unfocused effort which lacks any underpinning direction or driving force.

Strategy, like planning, applies at all levels: to the overall approach to communication, to full ongoing programmes and to individual campaigns. It's important because it focuses effort, it gets results and it looks to the long term.

WHAT IS STRATEGY?

Strategy is the cohering approach that is taken to a programme or campaign. It is the coordinating theme or factor, the guiding principle, the rationale behind the tactical programme.

Strategy is dictated by the issues arising from analysis of the information at the planners disposal (see Chapter 4). It is not the same as objectives and it comes before tactics. It is the foundation upon which a tactical programme is built. Strategy is the principle that will move the planner from where they are now to where they want to be. It is sometimes called 'the big idea'. Sometimes it is: it can be an all-embracing concept. Sometimes it isn't, and planners shouldn't be overly concerned if they can't come up with a big idea. They should, however, be very concerned if they don't have a clear rationale.

A very clear if unpleasant example of 'strategy' and 'tactics' was demonstrated in the war conducted by the combined forces which moved against Iraq following that country's invasion of Kuwait (a particularly appropriate example bearing in mind the military origins of the two words):

The objective:	to get the Iraqis out of Kuwait
The strategy:	according to General Colin Powell was to cut them (the Iraqis) off and kill them
The tactics:	pincer movement of ground forces to cut the Iraqis off from Iraq, carpet bombing, divisionary tactics, cutting bridges and so on

Further examples of the relationship between objectives, strategy and tactics are given in Table 7.1.

Strategies can be built around a number of propositions. For example, sometimes a strategy is clearly borne out of the necessity to use certain kinds of channels. If the issue is credibility, then endorsement by indirect channels (third partner) may be the strategy chosen. Sometimes the strategy is to focus on a particular theme or message. The long-running road safety campaigns in the UK revolve around the message, 'Think!' – think before you drink and drive; think by keeping distance between you and the driver in front; think about the results of speeding, etc.

In a nutshell, strategy is *how* you will achieve an objective and tactics are *what* you will do. For large programmes with several elements, eg community relations, employee relations and customer relations, there may well be strategy for each part of the programme.

FROM STRATEGY TO TACTICS

Tactics are the methods or activities that are used to implement the strategy.

Table 7.1 *Examples of objectives, strategy and tactics*

	Example one (single-objective, short-term campaign)	Example two (longer-term strategic positioning programme)
Objective	Publicize new product or service	Establish as market leader
Strategy	Mount media relations campaign in niche press	Position as industry voice of authority
Tactics	Press conference Press releases Interviews Competition Advertising etc	Research-based reports Quality literature Media relations Thought-leading website Speaker platforms Industry forums Award schemes etc

It goes without saying that tactics should be clearly linked to strategy. When developing a tactical programme all the powers of creativity need to be deployed, but there are one or two key factors that should be borne in mind:

- *Use strategy to guide brainstorms.* Strategy should not act as a strait-jacket, but it does help to keep focus on the job in hand.
- *Reject non-strategic activities.* Brainstorms are marvellous and stimulating, and all kinds of exciting ideas can emerge. However, no matter how good the idea, non-strategic activities should be discarded: if they don't fit in with the strategic thrust of this programme, they need to be put on one side.
- *Relate tactics to strategy and strategy to objectives.* There should be a definite logical progression. Objectives give the overall direction to the programme – what needs to be achieved. Strategy provides the driving force, the 'how to', and tactics give the activity programme in detail, what will be done on a day-to-day basis.
- *Test tactics where possible.* It is always advisable to find out as far as possible if a particular tactic will work. There may be a reasonable expectation it will work because similar things have been before, in a slightly different context. Test feasibility as far as possible. Thus, if the idea is to run a series of competitions in the regional press, there needs to be contact with two or three papers to find out if they are in sympathy with the idea.

The link between strategy and tractics is crucial and two things should be borne in mind. If the strategy has been carefully thought-through and it is clearly the right one to use, tactics should be changed before strategy. It is likely that something is wrong at the tactical level if a programme is not working as it should. Changing strategy means that there is probably something wrong at a fundamental level, maybe with the conclusions on the main issues or with the objectives that have been set, or maybe there is something missing in the analysis that has been done.

Of course, there must be some flexibility of approach. Sometimes when moving on to the tactics of a campaign it is realized that a particular tactic, or group of tactics, should become the strategic thrust of the programme. For example, maybe a company has a problem with name recognition (people remember the products but not the organization). It could well be that the strategy is to project the company name more prominently on its promotional material. Tactically, new literature is recommended that has stronger company branding together with a revamp of the website and making the company name larger on the products. Putting this into practice may lead the public relations professional to the conclusion that a rethink of the company's corporate identity is required, and this then becomes the strategy, giving coherence, direction and a framework around which to hang the communication programme as a whole.

While the classic way to plan is strategy firrt and then tactics, it is sometimes the case that some tactics just stand out as being obvious and should be core to the programme. For example, with scientific communities evidence is required, hence research-based activities are an obvious tactic. Back-rationalizing this thinking could lead to the planner concluding that a strategy based on a number of research reports on key issues is correct. Tactics would then focus on the exploitation of these reports and associated activities.

WHAT TACTICS SHOULD BE EMPLOYED?

It would be easy to think up a series of clever ideas and put them together into some kind of programme. Too often the techniques themselves become the focus of attention rather than the objective they are meant to achieve.

A programme with a variety of publics and objectives will need a variety of tactics.

One way of looking at public relations programmes is to regard them as 'contact and convince' or 'contact and dialogue' programmes. The first task is to identify and contact the relevant target publics, which entails selecting the publics and choosing a channel of communication through which to contact them. Second, convince them, through the power of communications, that they should think, believe or act in a certain way, or set up the platform for dialogue.

The set of techniques used in a contact programme must reach the requisite number of target publics and get the desired content across to them with enough impact so as to influence them in some way. And this must be done at a reasonable cost. So the public relations practitioner needs to select from a menu of activities of the kind shown in Figure 7.1.

Careful choices have to be made about the combination of techniques to be used and the balance between the various activities selected. Each technique has its own strengths and weaknesses. The idea is to select a range of techniques that complement each other and which, when taken as a whole, provide a powerful raft of communication.

Some examples will illustrate the point. If a company wants to launch a new and highly visual product, such as a new range of expensive cosmetics, it is important that techniques are selected that allow the physical qualities of the product to be demonstrated and where there is some opportunity for some two-way communication. Techniques employed might be an interactive website, exhibitions, sending product samples to journalists and specialist interest online sites and communities, brochures with high-quality photographs and a coupon response that can be followed up by sending samples, a campaign with specialist magazines with product samples attached for consumers, sampling opportunities at retail outlets, and demonstrations at fashion events.

In another situation, say where a company chairperson wants to give detailed financial information to some key investors, the visual and tactile aspects would not be so important, neither is the chairperson talking to a mass audience. In this instance it is important that the message is closely controlled, so an on- and offline mass media campaign would not be the best method. The methods chosen might be seminars, production of detailed briefings and one-to-one or small group meetings. In these instances, the opportunity for one-to-one interaction to check understanding and support would be critical.

Sometimes the type of campaign clearly dictates the selection of techniques. It would be a brave (or foolish) car manufacturer who did not take its new model to motor shows and allow journalists to test drive it.

Likewise, some techniques are more appropriate to certain types of campaigns. In the consumer area stunts and attention-grabbing, creative ideas that can be used with the media or online are often a part of the programme, but this is not usually the case in serious lobbying campaigns (although sometimes it is).

The Central Office of Information (COI) have developed a method for determining tactics based on the stakeholder mapping techniques given in Chapter 6. The thinking behind the method is that those with most power and interest require most attention, and that communication should be personalized and designed to engage them. Those with least power and interest should have least attention devoted to them, the techniques should

MEDIA RELATIONS	INTERNAL COMMUNICATION
Press conference Press releases Articles and features One-to-one briefings Interviews Background briefings/materials Photography Letters to editors Story ideas Advertorials Guest editorials Media directories Video news releases Website E-mail	Videos Briefings Newsletters Quality guides CD/DVD E-mail Intranet Business tv Meetings One-to-ones
ADVERTISING	CORPORATE IDENTITY
Corporate and product Magazines Nespapers Websites TV, cable, radio Billboard posters Signage Merchandise	Logos Buildings Product branding Clothing Letterheads Publications Website Merchandise Vehicles
DIRECT MAIL	SPONSORSHIP
Annual report Brochures/leaflets Customer reports External newsletters General literature Merchandise CD/DVD Letters	Sport Arts Worthy causes Education
EXHIBITIONS	LOBBYING
Trade and Public Literature Sampling Demonstrations	One-to-one briefings Background material Literature Group briefings

Multimedia	Hospitality
	CD and DVD
	Audio cassettes
CONFERENCES	RESEARCH
Multimedia	Organizations
Literature	Public relations programmes
Hospitality	Issues monitoring
	Results monitoring
COMMUNITY RELATIONS	CRISIS MANAGEMENT
Direct involvement	Planning
Gifts-in-kind	Implementation
Sponsorship	
Donations	
SPECIAL EVENTS	LIAISON
AGMs	Internal (including counselling)
SGMs	External
Special occasions	
Fairs	
Carnivals	
Social events	
Fundraising	
CUSTOMER RELATIONS	FINANCIAL RELATIONS
Media relations	Annual report
Direct mail	Briefing materials
Advertising	One-to-one briefing
Internet	Media relations
Social networks	Hospitality
Exhibitions	Internet
Retail outlets	Extranet
Sponsorship	
Product literature	
Newsletters	

Figure 7.1   *Range of tactics available to practitioners*

be less personal (mass) and engagement is not important. Figure 7.2 provides the strategy (headings in bold) with example tactics for the power interest matrix.

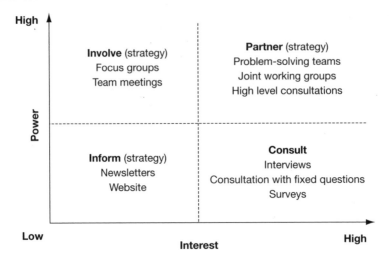

Figure 7.2 *COI methodology for linking strategy and tactics*

However, there is a danger with this approach as indicated in Chapter 6. Those people with low interest and low power may be exactly the kind of individuals with whom an organization wishes to engage; therefore by using more interactive and personal communication, attempts can be made to stimulate engagement with them.

Clearly there is an enormous range or tactics available, so how is the final selection made? There are two tests to apply:

- *Appropriateness.* Will the technique actually reach the target publics being aimed for? Will they have the right amount of impact? Is this a credible and influential technique to carry the message the organization is waiting to relay? Will the message get through using this technique? Do the techniques suit the message (content, tone, creative treatment)? Is it compatible with other communication devices that the organization is using?
- *Deliverability.* Can these techniques be implemented successfully? Can it be done within the budget and to the required timescale? Is there access to the right people with the right expertise to implement the techniques?

Having made the decisions about which broad techniques to employ, consideration has to be given to the specific media to use. Thus, if it is decided that an exhibition is a most suitable technique, then ask which exhibition needs to be attended. Here judgements have to be made on areas such as how many target publics attend the list of available exhibitions. There may be a particular sub-set that needs contacting. How does the cost compare between the different exhibitions and which is most cost-effective? What sort of fellow exhibitors will there be and are they likely to enhance or detract from the organization's reputation? How influential are those exhibitions? Can the organization afford not to be there? Who is of importance, for example the media, and will they be there? What are the logistical practicalities of attending one as opposed to another exhibition?

It is in the area of tactics that creativity can shine. A good creative idea adds sparkle and difference to a campaign, and it doesn't have to be entirely wacky either. A nice example is provided by a residential care community looking after adults with long-term mental health and physical disability problems. The members of the community are virtually self-sufficient and a key part of their working lives centres on a farm. To encourage support, the community sends out packs of postcards, showing, in high-quality photographs, the life and surroundings of community members and how they are doing all they can to help themselves. It is a simple and effective way for the community to encourage others to support their work.

DIFFERENT CAMPAIGNS NEED DIFFERENT TACTICS

To illustrate different approaches using very different techniques, here are three detailed case studies. All the campaigns have been successful – they won CIPR Excellence Awards – but they were aimed at very different audiences and therefore required quite different treatments.

Vargo, the first guide dog to enter a mosque: Guide Dogs for the Blind Association

The Islamic faith has many sensitivities about dogs, only recognizing them for guarding and hunting, not as pets in the home. As a result the Guide Dogs for the Blind Association (GDBA) were receiving reports of Muslim taxi drivers and other service providers refusing guide dog owners access to their services as they often misunderstood what guide dogs do and how clean they are.

So the GDBA and the Muslim Council of Britain (MCB) agreed to work together to promote mutual understanding and highlight how guide dogs help their visually impaired owners.

The campaign started in November 2007 when an event was held for the Muslim community to increase awareness of how guide dogs help their owners and that the dogs have high standards of grooming and cleanliness. Mahomed Abraar, a 17-year-old visually impaired Muslim from Leicester, and his father Gafar attended and asked if Mahomed could have a guide dog.

His story was used to highlight the fact that guide dogs are working animals who can greatly enhance a person's independent mobility. To allow Mahomed complete freedom with his guide dog, an historic fatwa was issued to allow him to take his guide dog to his mosque for daily worship. This change in ancient Shari'ah law meant that, on 24 September 2008, Vargo became the first guide dog in the UK to enter a mosque.

Objectives

- gain national media coverage of the first guide dog in the UK to ever enter a mosque;
- raise awareness of the change in Shari'ah law and the fact this now applied world-wide;
- help build support in the local community for Mahomed having a guide dog;
- help promote and increase guide dog ownership amongst visually-impaired Muslims;
- raise awareness of how GDBA tailors its services to individuals' needs.

Audiences

- GDBA staff, volunteers and guide dog owners;
- local community in Leicester;
- Muslim community in Leicester and UK;
- Muslim community throughout the world.

Strategy

Use one iconic event to demonstrate that guide dog ownership was acceptable in the Muslim community.

Tactics

Media targets:

- GDBA targeted the national print, broadcast and online media, particularly those with a large Muslim audience (for example BBC Asian Network, The Muslim News);
- local media were also targeted in order to encourage the Muslim community to support this event;
- specific-interest press were targeted to highlight the joint working between GDBA and MCB to promote mutual understanding.

Media relations:

- all the national media were targeted and the release included translation of the historic fatwa and quotes of support from senior figures in the Muslim community;
- photocall/filming opportunity issued to capture the event;
- interview opportunities with Mahomed, his father, local mosque leaders and Vargo's trainer from GDBA were arranged;
- photos of the landmark moment were distributed by newswires nationally and internationally.

Evaluation

- This campaign exceeded expectations for coverage, featuring in *The Times*, *The Guardian*, *Channel 4 News*, BBC Radio 2 and 4 news, BBC *Radio 5 live*, BBC *Asian Network*, BBC Arabic service, *The Asian Today* and *The Muslim News*.
- BBC Radio 4's *In Touch*, and *You and Yours* programmes were devoted entirely to this story. ITV Central (East and West) and BBC East Midlands TV covered the story on all their bulletins before the event and on the day. Over 60 pieces of print and online coverage appeared in the UK and internationally (objective 1).
- New, positive links have been forged between GDBA and the Muslim community. GDBA has since received applications from four visually-impaired Muslims who heard the story and in 2009 GDBA began work to build on this achievement by further increasing awareness of its services in this community (objective 4).
- The fatwa and Mahomed Abraar and Vargo's story has set a precedent, encouraging other blind and partially sighted Muslims to consider guide dog ownership.
- It has paved the way for mosque leaders both in the UK and internationally to make similar adjustments to enable Muslim guide dog owners to enter their mosque (objectives 2, 3, 4).
- GDBA used this story to highlight the fact that guide dogs are working animals enhancing a person's independence and was a massive step forward for other blind and partially sighted Muslims (objectives 3, 4).
- Guide dog schools in Turkey, Abu Dhabi and the Philippines are using this landmark judgment as a precedent to help visually impaired people in those countries apply for guide dogs (objectives 2, 4, 5).

Points about the campaign

- This was potentially a controversial campaign that challenged customs and practices among the Muslim community. The partnership with the Muslim Council of Britain was vital to gaining support and to mitigate the attendant risks.
- There were in effect two key elements to the campaign: change Shari'ah law and demonstrate that the law had changed in a very powerful way. Using Vargo's entry to the mosque was a 'killer' strategy. All opposition and fears were addressed by this one highly symbolic act.
- Changing the world does not mean that a huge budget is required. The strategy was simple, effective and low cost: under £1,000.
- The single tactic of a media event was a catalyst for a chain of reactions that will each have their own 'lives' and will perpetuate the effects of the campaign.

The Pipers' Trail: Golley Slater's campaign for the Army in Scotland

For centuries, the links between Scottish communities and the Army have been strong. The strength of community spirit and the pride and passion Scots have for their regiments has been entrenched in a rich and powerful heritage that few nations can emulate.

However, at a time when many Scottish soldiers were engaged in Operations overseas, the presence of the Army in local communities throughout Scotland was dwindling. The most obvious impact of this has been a decline in recruitment numbers stretching back over five years.

The Army recruited Golley Slater to ensure that it remains a positive, supported element in Scottish life.

Client objectives

- reconnect the Army's role and relationship with Scottish local communities;
- communicate the Army's core values and standards;
- increase recruitment numbers from Scotland;
- achieve a Return on Investment of 1:10 in terms of positive media coverage.

Target audience

- local communities throughout Scotland.

Strategy

Use the Army standards in and values of community and educational engagement to reconnect with communities. The main vehicle for this was a suggestion by Brigadier David Allfrey, Commander, 51 (Scottish) Brigade who had the vision of The Pipers' Trail, a 470-mile musical journey through Scotland led by the Army pipers and drummers and volunteers. The Trail would be used as a means to refocus positive attention on the Army and assist it in engaging more fully with Scottish society, thus reinforcing its position with local communities.

Tactics

Media engagement:

Before the Piper's Trail started Golley Slater organized a pre-launch photocall in May 2008 in Glasgow to inform all Scottish media that it was taking place. This was supplemented by diary notes sent to all national and regional media with details of what was happening in their area as the Trail weaved its way through Scotland.

Press packs were issued containing details on key individuals taking part in the Trail along with detailed maps of the 470 mile route highlighting dates and timings of when The Pipers' Trail would arrive in each location as well as timings of the workshops and the play associated with it.

As the Trail was launched in a very remote part of Scotland (most northerly tip of Shetland) pre-recorded interviews were prepared, which went live on the day. The Army's own press photographer attended, who in turn issued photographs of the launch to Scottish media.

The Army had one of its own press officers on the ground for the duration of the Trail. They felt that in order to maximize publicity an army representative was needed who could feed quirky stories to the media, as well as providing a voice on the ground when The Pipers arrived in the towns and cities. This would prepare for any adverse media coverage to be handled following the Army protocol.

In addition, the agency engaged with the media by alerting journalists working on forward planning desks, preparing creative ideas for features, organizing broadcast interviews and providing listings for 'what's-on' pages as the Trail made its way through Scotland.

Community engagement:

For The Pipers' Trail to succeed it needed the support from local communities along the route. The engagement programme included:

- Piping and Drumming Workshops: Engagement with locals allowing them to try first hand the pipes and drums and take part in The Pipers' Trail.
- Marching Pipes and Drums: A pipe band would perform to locals with added musical support from those who took part in the workshops.
- The Pipers' Trail Play: A 45 minute musical play incorporating the Army's key messages performed in local communities along the Trail. And in a 'first', the Army took the play to the Edinburgh Fringe which performed for 12 days.
- Veterans' Day: Linking in with local Veteran Day parades along the route, The Pipers' Trail joined and led marches throughout Scotland.
- The website: The website www.thepiperstrail.com was used as the portal for workshop registration, providing news updates, promoting real-time geographical locations of the pipers and providing locals with images taken from the start to the finish of The Pipers' Trail.

Educational engagement:

Forty different towns, villages and cities were visited as the route was piped and drummed by the Army and civilian volunteers. A unique element of The Pipers' Trail was the inclusion of the theatrical play that told the story of a teenage boy and his own musical journey across Scotland. This piece of theatre was performed in village squares as well as town and city centres along the route. Featured heavily in the play was the Army's core values of selfless commitment, courage, discipline, integrity, loyalty and respect for others.

The Trail also encouraged widespread national support by inviting people to get involved and either join or follow the pipers along the Trail. Amateur and professional pipers, drummers and pipe bands of all ages and standards were encouraged to study and play together and take part in the Trail. For the Pipers' Trail to be a success it was important that it connected with locals, so for those who wished to take part, but who had little or no piping and drumming experience, four-day piping and drumming workshops were held prior to the Trail arriving in their town.

Online PR

To supplement these tactics there was an innovative use of online PR through social networking websites.

The www.thepiperstrail.com website was designed, built and managed on a daily basis by the Golley Slater team and was critical to the success of The Pipers' Trail. The media were encouraged to publicize the web address and it was utilized by the general public who could find out more information on the Trail, with event dates, timings, locations, maps as well as a section that allowed the public to view photographs and videos of past events. This site acted as the hub for all the other online services, which included Bebo, Facebook, Flickr, Youtube and Google Maps.

Bebo: www.bebo.com/thepiperstrail08

A branded Bebo page was set up so that people could add The Pipers' Trail as one of their favourite bands and become a 'fan'. The profile also allowed event listings and songs to be posted. Photos of events were regularly uploaded, 'Pipers' Trail TV' videos were added to the profile, blog updates were posted with news, and the 'say something' box was updated daily with details of what was happening on the Trail that day.

The profile was monitored several times a day and all visitor comments required approval before appearing on the profile. Despite this, no negative comments were ever made by any visitor to the profile. Overall, the Bebo site proved very successful and in turn drove a large amount of traffic to the official site.

Facebook: http://www.facebook.com/pages/The-Pipers-Trail/21169074026

A branded Facebook band page was set up so that people could add The Pipers' Trail as one of their favourite bands and become a 'fan'. The band profile also allowed event listings and songs to be posted. Photos of events were uploaded, and 'the wall' box was updated regularly with details of what was happening on the Trail that day. The profile was monitored daily and all visitor comments required approval before appearing on the profile.

Flickr: www.flickr.com/photos/25887450@N06/

A Pipers' Trail profile was set up to store all photos of events on the Trail. Details were added to the photos, such as The Pipers' Trail web address, crown copyright notice, general category tags, and geo-tags with the town/city they were taken in. They were also grouped into sets according to the area they were taken in, for ease of navigation. Whenever new photos were uploaded, the 'latest photos' box at the bottom of thepiperstrail.com index page was automatically updated.

Evaluation

- Media coverage: a total of £1.25 million AVE, covering weekly, regional and national press and broadcast was achieved (objective 4);
- a total of 116 press cuttings were generated, 102 were from local media outlets thereby achieving the aim of the Army linking in with local communities (objective 1);
- similarly, 38 broadcast pieces were generated, 30 of which were with local TV and radio stations (objective 1);
- 10 minute interview with Brigadier Allfrey on Newsnight Scotland reiterating key messages (objective 2);
- key messages were present in 97 per cent of media coverage;

- in seven weeks, The Pipers' Trail website had 12,185 unique visitors with 71,014 page views (objective 1);
- attendance at the piping and drumming workshops was in excess of 1,000;
- circa 250,000 people watched The Pipers' Trail and saw the play along the route (objectives 1, 2);
- approximately 3,000 attended the Edinburgh Fringe event (objective 2);
- recruitment figures for 2008–2009 (at time of writing) show an 8 per cent year-on-year increase (objective 3);
- on the back of the success of The Pipers' Trail, the Army organized a similar event in Scotland as part of Homecoming Scotland 2009 (objectives 1, 2).

Points about the campaign

- The campaign had a single, strong co-ordinating theme: the Pipers' Trail, which was used to demonstrate the Army's values and engage with the local communities: an effective strategy.
- The campaign was fun and different as well as being educational.
- It successfully tapped into a strong and emotional tradition – piping.
- The focus was on personal engagement: the target publics could meet, dance with and talk to the Army who successfully drew people into a 'community' with them.
- The additional twist of the play added an unusual element for getting across the Army's key messages.

SUSTAINING LONG-TERM PROGRAMMES

One of the key issues in longer-term public relations programmes is sustainability. How is a programme kept going year after year maintaining focus and interest? Running an event with a single, short-term objective that is achieved in a determined timescale, eg holding a Christmas party for employees and their families, is rather different from sustaining a long-running programme on financial advice.

Here is an example of a long-running programme that has 'rolled-out' over many years.

Lansons Communications campaign for IFA Promotion Ltd ('Unbiased.co.uk'), the organization representing Britain's independent financial advisors

In 1993 Lansons Communications began a new approach to IFA Promotion's marketing strategy. A year-long campaign called 'Tax-Action' focused on the £8 billion paid every year in unnecessary tax. The solution was for people to use Independent Financial Advisors (IFAs) to get the correct professional financial advice. IFA Promotion ran a consumer hotline that gave callers the names and addresses of their three nearest IFAs.

The campaign was a great success and responses to the hotline increased by 160 per cent.

The task in 1994 was to build upon the success of the previous year, to convince more ABC1s to use professional advisors and to contact the hotline. Promoting independent financial advice as the preferred route and convincing IFAs to run marketing initiatives based on IFA Promotion's lead was an ongoing objective.

The new campaign was designed to keep the best of 'Tax Action' and to broaden its appeal. It also aimed to add to the theme. 'Britain's Undiscovered Billions' looked at all the money wasted each year through financial mismanagement or inertia. Two new types of waste apart from tax were highlighted: 'dead money', the focus being missed return because money not needed day to day is left idle (often in current accounts); and 'buried treasure', money that is rightfully ours but left unclaimed, eg from legacies, premium bonds and state benefits.

The underpinning of Undiscovered Billions was research done by Mintel that quantified the waste. This research was based on the analysis of the Inland Revenue's own 'Personal Income Survey', which gives an in-depth analysis of 70,000 individual cases. Additional data were obtained from the Target Group Index survey conducted by BMRB International (British Market Research Bureau) among 25,000 adults each year, and other conclusions were based on industry analysis. The research discovered that in 1994 British people could have been £12 billion better off – an average of £300 per adult – if only they had managed their finances better.

Lansons used the research as a platform both for a national and media campaign and a local marketing campaign run by IFAs. Following the launch, the Mintel figures were used to launch 12 separate public relations initiatives. These mini-campaigns, rolled out at a rate of two per month, covered topics such as holiday currency money wasted by not shopping around for insurance.

Lansons also put together a 'case studies' database of people helped by IFAs for use by the press (150 IFAs country-wide co-operated). Video news release footage based on real-life case studies was also prepared and an advertorial campaign, run with the Newspaper Society, was taken up by over 100 regional newspapers. The IFAs themselves came to training seminars, where they were given guidance on using a marketing pack containing adverts, draft client letters, posters, case studies, a summary of the Mintel finding and a copy of the *Money Detector* booklet that was given out free when people contacted the hotline.

The results of the 1994/95 campaign were exceptional. In the first five months of the campaign, 46,500 people contacted the IFA Promotion hotline, up by 58 per cent from 1993, and over 40,000 people requested the *Money Detector* booklet.

IFA Promotion's annual Gallup monitoring survey showed that 56 per cent of ABC1 adults were likely to go to IFAs for advice. Recognition of the blue IFA logo went up from 41 to 52 per cent. Over 75 per cent of IFA Promotion's 4,000-strong membership took part in the 'Tax Action' campaign.

Every national newspaper bar one covered the campaign in its first two weeks. The BBC made a programme called *Here and Now* based on the issues, using IFA Promotion material. The theme they developed was 'Taxbusters'. The findings were also featured in the BBC's *Good Fortunes* programme. The IFA Promotion's chief executive was interviewed by 30 radio stations.

So, how can the momentum of such a successful programme be maintained over subsequent years?

The 'Tax Action' theme has provided the backbone of Lansons' work for IFA Promotion and has ensured a constant level of media coverage. Tax is a recurring theme in the lives of every adult each year and Lansons are able to capitalize on this, publishing the findings of IFA Promotion's 'Tax Action' investigation annually. The results are regionalized to give local as well as national media appeal. For example, the 2009 investigation revealed that nearly 2.6 million people in Wales unnecessarily paid £481 million, either through inertia or because of lack of understanding of the taxation rules.

Having a long-term theme does not mean that the programme is simply an updating process. According to Lansons, the opportunity is now taken to capitalize on the financial issues of the moment and those that they can predict. So in 2009, the depth of recession, they revealed that 72 per cent of adults expected their tax burden to rise that year, as well as revealing the nation's most resented taxes: the Council Tax, TV licence (41 per cent) and fuel duty. This and other consumer research angles were used throughout the year to support the core Wasted Tax report and strengthen the 'see an IFA' message.

Over recent years, the public relations campaign has shifted its focus significantly to reflect IFA Promotion's evolving business strategy. Having moved in 2007 to become an online only service, under the Unbiased.co.uk brand, all of the organization's focus is now on driving traffic to this website to Find an IFA. To this end, Lansons seeks to generate the lion's share of IFA Promotion's profile online, supplementing this with continued campaign coverage in the traditional broadcast and print media.

As well as targeting online news media for coverage of the monthly Tax Action stories, Lansons produces and pitches 'white label' content to IFA Promotion's established network of over 60 content partner websites. These include news media sites such as Telegraph.co.uk, Times Online and FT.com, internet portals such as MSN, AOL and Tiscali, and specialist sites such as MyMoneyDiva and MoneyMagpie.

In 2008, the team placed 42 items of white label content across these sites, including interactive tax calculators, podcasts and full Tax Action microsites. The 2009 Tax Action campaign was launched with a webchat, white-labelled across 15 media sites, giving the public the chance to quiz an IFA on ways to save tax. During the launch week, the webchat attracted more than 5,000 visitors.

This early shift to content production and placement has given the Tax Action campaign a valuable extra dimension. By creating interactive content around the core Find an IFA facility, Lansons has been able to boost the campaign's reach and stand out, engaging with consumers more directly and personalizing an already successful media campaign.

Points about the campaign

- Identifying a thorny issue (tax) that is a feature of every working adult's life and which has an annual focus (the tax return) ensures a built-in interest.
- Because people are interested in the issue, so are the media.
- Making material as pertinent as possible to individuals is vitally important; use of regional media is a major tactic.
- The internet extends the media opportunities for a campaign, but it can offer much more, especially for a brand with a strong online proposition. Campaigns can be made interactive and personal, increasing the range and depth of audience engagement with the topic.

- Capitalizing on issues of the moment – and of tomorrow – keeps the role of the IFAs to the front of people's minds throughout the year, not just when the tax return is done. It also helps to set the media agenda by indicating those issues that will be of interest in the near future.
- The role of public relations is to generate awareness and interest, not to sell individual products, which is a job best left to the regulated experts.
- A long-term successful public relations campaign must continually evolve, to reflect how audiences consume information, refresh their interest, and take account of changes to broader business or marketing strategy.

CONTINGENCY AND RISK PLANNING

All good public relations plans cater for the unexpected. There isn't room in this book to go into the whole area of crisis management. That subject, along with issues management, is dealt with in *Risk Issues and Crisis Management in Public Relations*, another book in this series.

Contingency planning

However, it is necessary to be prepared for the unexpected at both the strategic and tactical levels. Strategic-level threats are those that have the potential to fatally or very seriously damage the organization. At the strategic level a contingency plan is needed for a number of possibilities, for example:

- if the reputation of the organization is badly damaged;
- if its financial position is jeopardized;
- if its ability to function is interrupted;
- if its supporters desert it;
- if the public decides its operations are no longer legitimate.

These are major crises requiring a considered response that needs planning. Examples of activities that might precipitate such a crisis are new or proposed legislation, life-threatening competitor activity, product withdrawal, an acquisition or takeover, strikes, an act of terrorism, a factory closure or heavy redundancies, suspect trading activities or operating in a sector that is no longer seen to be acceptable.

In some of these situations tightening up on quality control, improving industrial relations or improving the quality of intelligence-gathering processes could help prevent problems becoming crises. It is the public relations professional's job to look out for the possible problem areas and to ensure that there are plans in place to deal with the communication implications. It is rare for issues to arise out of the blue, but there are many examples of organizations who have not recognized the warning signs. It will be necessary to liaise with other key people in the organization such as the chief executive, marketing function, sales/distribution, finance and quality areas, not to mention the lawyers and insurance advisers. It will also often be necessary to liaise with external bodies such as regulators, valued partners and trade associations in preparation for strategic threat management.

The public relations professional's tasks will probably include:

- planning for potential crises with others in the company and possibly external bodies;
- helping to put together a crisis management team, training them and ensuring there is clear communication between members;
- allocating responsibilities to crises team members;
- putting together the crisis plan;
- initiating 'trial-runs' of the plan;
- keeping the plan up to date;
- training key members of staff to handle the media and other key stakeholders;
- ensuring media enquiries are planned for and that there is suitable back-up;
- putting together key policy statements;
- acting as a part of the crisis management team if required;
- learning from the crises to improve contingency plans.

Of course, at the strategic level, each of the various scenarios will need to be considered in its own right and a separate plan of action developed. There will be common areas in each plan, such as the process for dealing with media, but tailor-made solutions are required for events of such importance.

At the tactical level contingency planning follows the same principles, but the degree to which these principles are applied will vary. For example, a crisis team may not be needed, but there will need an individual to take responsibility. This requires a careful examination of each tactic in the programme to find out what might go wrong. Thus, if an outdoor event is planned, what happens if the weather is bad? What if there are accidents or incidents at the event? What if some of the equipment fails? A balance has to be struck between the ideal and the realistic. If a fireworks show has been arranged another display cannot be ready just in case, but the performance record of the supplier will have been checked, and one part of the display may be kept in reserve and used at the end if all goes to plan. Certainly the organizer will ensure that there are umbrellas available or a covered stand so that people are kept dry.

Risk

A topic related to contingency, but preceding it is risk. If risks are identified then contingencies must be put in place. Risks are those threats, sometimes hidden, but sometimes known about, that may place the organization in jeopardy in some way. Professional public relations planners always undertake a thorough risk assessment of their programme at all stages, but particularly with certain elements.

Key areas of risk always need careful assessment, such as the publics that are being worked with and the tactics that are employed. With publics there can be risk attached to who the programme is being targetted at: are they the right people, are there any unintended consequences that might occur? If so, how serious will the impact be?

There can be a risk associated with using certain individuals or organizations as partners. Celebrities can turn out to be liabilities, or behave in ways that do not promote the product. For example, a celebrity may be paid to promote a certain brand of clothing, but be seen to be frequently wearing another brand. Similarly, an organization that appeared to be the perfect partner, such as a campaigning group, may discover other aspects of the business with which they are unhappy and decide to withdraw co-operation, with all the attendant difficulties that will create.

Turning to tactics, there are some that are inherently more dangerous than others – for example stunts or events involving large crowds. Other tactics may seem less risky, but could be found to be otherwise. For example it could be that a new website has all kinds of innovative features about it, but because of the type of imaging it uses, it may induce epilepsy.

Risk is not assessed necessarily to remove it, but to make the planner aware of its extent and likelihood. These two parameters are often used to plot risk, as Figure 7.3 shows.

Using this grid can help the planner decide whether the risk is acceptable. If the likelihood of a risk event happening is very high (nearer five on the likelihood scale) and its adverse impact on reputation or on a key relationship is also high (nearer five on the impact scale), then it could be that the planner will decide not to work with that organization or use that tactic. If the likelihood is high, but the impact is low, then that may be a risk worth taking. If the likelihood of a risk event happening is low, but the impact will be high, again a judgement will have to be made about whether to go ahead. Of course, if likelihood and impact are low, then risk is low.

One other thing to note. The risk grid implies that impact is negative. Of course impact can be positive. In this case instead of it being a risk tool, it can be turned into an opportunity tool to judge which tactics should be given the greatest priority.

Planning the strategy and tactics of a campaign is fun. It is challenging and demanding, both intellectually and creatively, but there is something

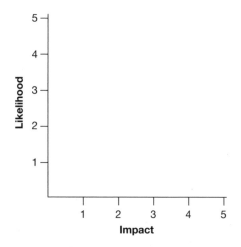

Figure 7.3 *A risk assessment tool*

uniquely rewarding about planning and then executing a programme that is well thought out and well judged. Good public relations plans are the result of much hard work and consideration. To come up with a strategy that works requires a great deal of research and incisive thinking to get to the heart of the matter. Tactics, too, should be chosen not just because they are imaginative, but also because they are appropriate to the publics towards whom they are directed and because they are without doubt the correct medium to carry the message.

Planning with care puts the practitioner in control. It enhances the probability of success and it ensures that the right things are focused on.

Note

1. For further information see Gregory, A (2007) Involving stakeholders in developing corporate brands: the communication dimension, *Journal of Marketing Management*, **23**, pp 59–73.

8

Timescales and resources

TIMESCALES

Two things are certain in a public relations practitioner's life. The first is that there is never enough time to do everything that needs to be done – the tasks and possibilities for action are always far greater than the time available. The second is that because public relations tasks often involve other people and the co-ordination of several elements, it always takes longer than you thought to get the job done.

There are two interlinked key factors that must be observed when considering timescales. The first is that deadlines must be agreed so that the tasks associated with a project can be completed on time. The second is that the right resources need to be allocated so that the tasks in hand can be completed. Timescales can be brought forward if more resources are brought in to complete the task.

Deadlines can be internally or externally imposed. Examples of internally imposed deadlines might be company keynote events such as the announcement of the chief executive's retirement; the announcement of an acquisition; the diaries of the people who might be involved in the public relations programme.

Externally imposed deadlines might be involvement in fixed events such as major shows and occasions like the Boat Show or the Summer Paralympic Games. There might be calendar dates that have to be worked to like Chinese New Year or Valentine's Day. Then there may be what would be regarded as most appropriate dates. Ideally new garden products would be launched in the spring when most people start to work in their gardens, but technically they could be launched at any time.

So how does the planner ensure that deadlines are met? The key thing is to identify all the individual tasks that have to be done in order for a project to be completed. Below is a list of the main elements of a straightforward press conference:

- Create invitation list.
- Investigate and organize venue.
- Book catering.
- Issue invitations.
- Book multimedia equipment.
- Write speeches.
- Prepare presentation materials.
- Prepare media packs.
- Follow up invitations.
- Prepare final attendance list.
- Rehearsals.
- Attend conference.
- Follow up.

Each of these elements then needs breaking down further into their component parts. Thus, for example, a fairly simple press pack might have in it a press release, some background briefing material, photographs, some product literature or a brochure and a specially designed press folder. To put the pack together will include briefing and monitoring designers, printers and photographers, writing the press material, liaising with the marketing department to get the product literature, liaising with senior management to get approval for the material, reproducing the press release and background briefing, collating the press packs and organizing delivery to the conference.

TASK PLANNING TECHNIQUES

There are a number of ways that the information can be organized visually to help planning.

Gantt Charts

Gantt Charts list each element of the project and then assign a time to it. These are then organized on the chart to show overlapping tasks. Using the chart also identifies when there are times when too many tasks are required to be undertaken at once. It could be that by completing one self-contained task early or later, time can be freed up in busy periods. If this is not possible, additional resources may be needed to help.

A Gantt Chart for the press conference might look something like Figure 8.1.

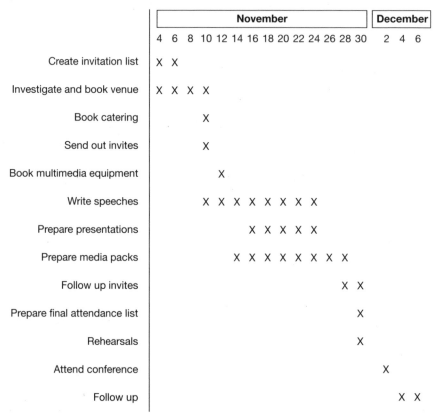

Figure 8.1 *Gantt Chart for press conference*

This particular chart involves some tasks that will need breaking down into smaller component parts. For example, the writing speeches task will involve a preliminary draft, initial approval and suggestions for alterations by the person delivering it, possibly CEO approval, redrafting, final approval, preparation of cue cards or auto cue, etc. This would be built into the Master chart. Similarly the press pack will have several elements too. A good practice is to allocate the names of the responsible people for the activities. Investigating and booking a venue may be outsourced to a specialist events agency and once they are briefed they should be able to get on with the task with minimal supervision. The media packs, as indicated earlier, will involve several individuals and possibly several companies and that requires greater project management. Responsibility lines must be very clear.

CRITICAL PATH ANALYSIS

An alternative method for time-lining projects in Critical Path Analysis (CPA)

Having split the project into its individual components, CPA requires the planner to identify those elements of a programme that involve the greatest amount of time. It is these elements that dictate when a project can be completed. CPA also recognizes that more than one task can be undertaken at a time and therefore enables participants to work as efficiently as possible. A critical path for our press packs is shown in Figure 8.2.

This represents a very tight timetable, and assumes that designers, printers and photographers are all available. Sometimes, of course, they are not. In practice most professionals will have a number of suppliers they can call on, and most projects do not begin from a standing start as shown in the example. However, the principle holds. Several things have to be done to put together a simple press pack, and they need to be carefully co-ordinated and timed with, preferably, a little contingency at the end (notice a whole day for collation and another one for delivery, with an intervening weekend) in case of emergencies. It is also good practice to get as much done as early as possible to give time at the end for any unforeseen problems. It would have been possible to brief the photographer on Day 4 and still have the prints back in time to collate the packs, but it would have been putting unnecessary pressure on the project.

Obviously, if pushed for time and there is a need to complete tasks earlier, ways must be sought to shorten some of the critical path activities. It may be, for example, that existing company folders are used to put press material in. Or it may be by allocating additional resources and paying the designer to work the weekend, a folder can be produced in a shortened timescale. If by shortening the crucial path as much as possible a fixed deadline cannot be met, the activity itself must be questioned and an alternative communication technique selected.

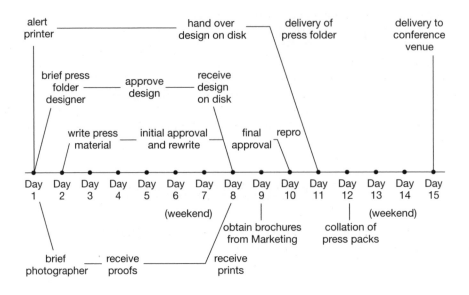

Figure 8.2 *Critical path for putting together a press pack*

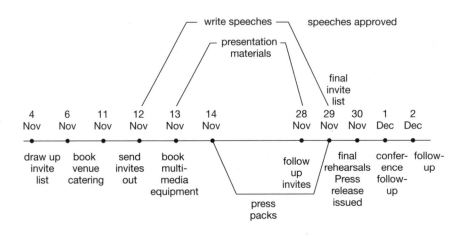

Figure 8.3 *Critical path for press conference*

Having once broken down the putting together of the press packs into its own critical path, this can then be put into the larger critical path for the press conference as a whole.

The final programme might look something like that shown in Figure 8.3. There are several project planning software programs now on the market that will produce automatic schedules and diary prompts, but the basic groundwork of deciding how long a task will take and who is involved will still have to be done, so understanding the principles behind techniques such as Gantt Charts and CPA is important.

It is vital that public relations practitioners manage their time effectively and work as efficiently as possible by having in place practices and procedures that regularize standard tasks, and by planning ahead. It is a mark of the professional manager. Another book in this series, *Public Relations: Practical Guide to the Basics* by Philip Henslowe, gives a range of checklists for typical public relations tasks such as event planning and specifications for suppliers. Checklists are the practitioner's friend and should be used to ensure that everything is covered and in the correct order.

LONGER-TERM PLANS

Putting together plans for individual projects is essential but if care is not taken the big picture is lost. It is absolutely critical that the multi-stranded programmes and the whole of the public relations department's activities are planned in as much detail as appropriate and an overall timetable for action is constructed. Many practitioners work to long-term objectives and may have outline plans for a number of years ahead. Getting those plans documented and approved is important because it helps maintain a focus beyond the immediate here and now. It is very easy to become so embroiled in day-to-day matters that the strategic vision becomes obscured and larger objectives become lost as the urgent takes over from the important.

Certainly, working to at least an annual plan is important. It helps to ensure that things happen when they are supposed to and it gives a level of control. If other activities arise, a judgement ca be made as to whether they or the planned activity should be pursued or if a case needs to be made for additional resources.

Overleaf is an example of an annual media campaign for a garden centre chain – see Table 8.1 on page 144. It is immediately apparent where the peaks of activity are. February, May and August are going to be heavy months, and it might be that extra resources are needed in the form of consultancy or freelance help.

Obviously, a large department or a consultancy carrying out comprehensive programmes will have several activity plans like this covering the

ACTIVITY	JAN	FEB	MAR	APR	MAY	JUN	JUL	AUG	SEP	OCT	NOV	DEC
Editor Briefings (one-to-one)	Trade press × 2 briefings	Consumer press × 2 briefings	Trade press × 2 briefings	Consumer press × 2 briefings	Trade press × 2 briefings							
Advertorials with key journals (to be negotiated)		House & Garden		Horticultural Journal		Garden Answers		Horticultural Week		Amateur Gardener		Royal Horticultural Society Journal
News Stories (including new products)	News story	Launch of lawncare advice service	New Centre opening	Launch of tree surgeon service	News story	New Centre opening	Barbecue promotion	News story	New Centre opening	Launch of new power tool range	Christmas plants promotion	New Centre opening
Seasonal themes (for regional press)	Tools		Spring is here		Care of fruit trees and bushes		Pest control		Care of borders		Winter lawncare	
Competitions with local press		Power tools promotion			Garden furniture promotion			Water features promotion			Indoor garden promotion	
Exhibitions with press reception					Chelsea Flower Show	Gardeners' World		Royal Horticultural Society				
Virtual press office	Web-site relaunch	Celebrity gardener video	Spring products	Gardening and youngsters	Celebrity gardener video	Summer planting	Water-saving tips	Celebrity gardener video	Gardening and the elderly	Late planting	Celebrity gardener video	Indoor decorations

Table 8.1 Annual planner for garden centre media campaign

whole gamut of public relations work. For example, they could well have an internal communications plan, a community relations plan, a business-to-business plan and several specific issues-based campaigns which will all need to be collated into a prioritized master plan. It is then that decisions on resources can be made. Either the plan will be accepted and resourced accordingly or, as is often the case, resources will be limited and therefore activities will have to be cut from the bottom of the priority list upwards. When making decisions on which areas are to be cut, great care has to be taken to ensure that the overall integrity of the campaigns or overall programmes of work are maintained and that what remains is a well-integrated campaign and overall programme that provide a good complementary raft of activities which will achieve the desired objectives and address all the essential publics.

Sheep Drive Over London Bridge: The Worshipful Company of World Traders

An example of meticulous logistical planning is the Worshipful Company of World Traders' public relations event to raise money for the 2008 Lord Mayor of London's Charity Appeal – an annual showcase occasion for the City of London.

Overview

Worshipful Companies are trade associations based in the City of London and are otherwise known as Livery Companies. The Livery Companies originally developed from the old Guilds who regulated the trades after which they were named and controlled such things as wages and conditions of labour. The Worshipful Company of World Traders is one of the newest Liveries and it wanted to create a notable project that would raise at least £40,000 for the Lord Mayor's Charity Appeal.

Money raised was to go to the Lord Mayor's two chosen charities, Wellbeing of Women – solving women's health problems in pregnancy, and Orbis – a worldwide blindness-prevention charity.

A team of five World Traders' Liverymen volunteers were chosen for their organizational, public relations and financial skills to run the seven-month campaign. The campaign proved highly complex involving liaising with many national and City of London authorities, coupled with the difficulties of dealing with livestock. The event itself proved to be one of the most high profile, colourful and fun events held in the City for years.

Campaign objectives

- raise a minimum of £40,000 for The Lord Mayor's charities;
- raise levels of awareness of Orbis and Wellbeing of Women to new business audiences;
- enhance the reputation of The World Traders among its peers as one of the newest Liveries.

Target publics

- approximately 3,000 Freemen;
- businesses in London;
- the public.

Campaign Strategy

To use an unusual and historic right of City of London Freemen as a platform to gain attention and raise funds for the Lord Mayor's Appeal and for the Livery.

All 3,000 Freemen of the city of London would be invited to re-enact their fabled 'right' to herd sheep across London Bridge. They would pay £50 each for the privilege and be encouraged to raise extra cash for the charities through additional sponsorship.

Having made this decision, the meticulous planning had to start.

The Sheep: A search for a flock of at least 15 sheep with a shepherd willing to participate was launched. Department of Environment, Food and Rural Affairs (DEFRA) movement of livestock regulations prevent the transfer of sheep between surveillance zones and made the task difficult. A herd was located in Kent – in the same zone as London. Of course, the idea of a flock of sheep being herded across London Bridge with no preparation was out of the question. The risk to animals, traffic and onlookers was potentially serious. So the sheep were trained to wear halters over their heads, and to become accustomed to City street noises by their trainers banging dustbin lids and shouting. The services of a qualified vet were enlisted to ensure the wellbeing of the sheep.

The Handlers: Representatives from Romney Sheep Breeders Society and students from Hadlow Agricultural College became sheep handlers on the day of the sheep drive.

The Bridge: London Bridge was selected after a major risk assessment of traffic and pedestrian issues.

Approvals Process: Before the event was announced approvals had to be gained from numerous organizations:

i) City of London Police

Police Authorities do not encourage initiatives such as this involving livestock. Traffic, livestock and people together usually cause problems. The attendance of the Lord Mayor and Lady Mayoress added another security issue. The event lighted the imagination of the Freemen of London, with 500 wanting to take part. That was double the number of expected participants, which meant that the event had to be extended from two hours to four and a half hours.

ii) DEFRA

DEFRA was in sole charge of the movement of livestock throughout the UK because of the threat of Blue Tongue disease. A licence for the movement of the sheep from Kent and within London had to be obtained.

iii) City of London Animal Health and Welfare Services

The overall care of the sheep was of paramount importance. A Welfare Officer attended two meetings to give guidance and a detailed risk assessment was prepared.

iv) City of London Street Cleansing
This proved to be an invaluable service throughout the Sheep Drive for obvious reasons!
v) City of London Corporation
The Corporation approved a street collection licence so that donations could be taken from onlookers.

Logistics of the Event

Apart from all the preparations mentioned earlier, for the event itself the plans were no less meticulous:

- The 261 metre London Bridge was divided into five, 50 metre stages. At each stage 15 Freemen herded 15 sheep in relays.
- A complex system of allocating places and time slots and informing 480 Liverymen who were driving sheep of their times of registration and positions on London Bridge, had to be planned in minute detail. The sheep and sheep handlers also had to be prepared and in position at the right times. Figure 8.4 shows the logistics plan for this.
- BlackRock Investment Management HQ building offered the only feasible pavement corral for the sheep on the day of the sheep drive.

The company agreed to help with:

- housing the sheep and providing food and water under its atrium;
- providing the sheep pens;
- providing parking for vehicles;
- arranging a conference room for media briefing;
- breakfast for media and farmers;
- lunch for 80 VIPs was provided by a City legal firm;
- the Red Cross provided medical cover free of charge;
- a jazz band attended free of charge to enhance the celebratory atmosphere;
- an additional Risk Assessment document was prepared to protect journalists and photographers from the unpredictable sheep, each weighing approximately 80 kilos!
- police, vets and street cleaning staff were all on hand to manage traffic, animals and hygiene as London Bridge was closed to vehicles during the sheep run.

Evaluation

- With GIFT AID more than £50,000 was raised for the Lord Mayor's Appeal.
- Orbis and Wellbeing of Women charities reached a wider audience through the publicity obtained.
- With the funds raised, Orbis established two specialist children's eye care centres in Rajasthan and trained two eye care teams to sustain eye care in poor local communities in India.
- Twenty-three journalists and photographers attended the event.
- Over a quarter-million pounds of press, broadcast and website coverage was generated.

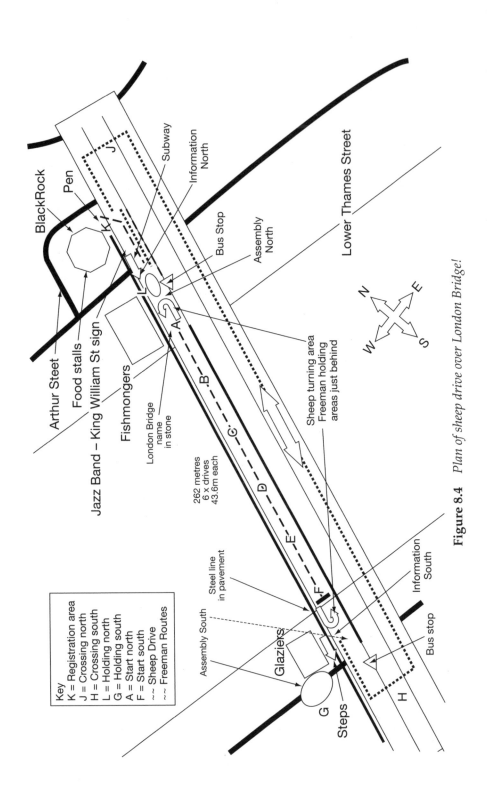

Figure 8.4 Plan of sheep drive over London Bridge!

- Coverage was worldwide and reached 12 million people.
- Public awareness was raised about the role of Livery Companies in The City of London.
- The World Traders gained credibility from other Livery Companies.
- The organizers of the event were guests of the Lord Mayor at a reception in Mansion House in November 2008 where a cheque for £48,680 was handed to the Lord Mayor. Additional funds followed.

Points about the campaign

- An event including animals adds significant complexity, involving several regulatory organizations and the need for extensive risk assessments. This all had to be factored into the time plans.
- The logistical detail required for this event was quite extraordinary; from time required to train the sheep, to obtaining the required permissions and licences, to organizing the City Freemen on London Bridge, to the welfare of the sheep on the day, to the stopping of traffic and so on. Each element needed its own risk assessment and plan of action that needed co-ordinating with the Master Plan.
- For events like these, communication among the organizing team is vital to prevent confusion and duplication of effort.
- Meticulous planning meant the event went off safely, without a hitch and great fun was had by all involved.

RESOURCES

Resourcing public relations adequately but effectively is of course necessary for organizational efficiency.

Resourcing of public relations programmes comes under three headings. The first is human resources, the second is operating or materials costs and the third is equipment.

Human resources

Whether working in-house or in consultancy the time and skills of individuals have to be paid for. The more experienced and adept the individual, the more expensive he or she is. Clearly the level of human resourcing depends on two things: the size of the programme that is to be undertaken and the nature of the programme.

There are tasks that most competent public relations practitioners would be expected to perform. For example, most would be expected to be able to run a media relations programme and produce literature of a good standard. However, highly complex lobbying or social networking programmes demand rarer skills and for that you will pay a premium.

A public relations professional with adequate administrative and equipment support can run a reasonably broad-based programme of limited depth. Alternatively he or she can handle a highly focused in-depth programme. The more comprehensive and multi-layered the programme, the more human resources will be required to run it, and the greater the levels of skill and experience needed.

In an ideal world an optimum programme is devised and justified, and the human resources required allocated. More realistically there is a trade-off between the ideal and the human resource overhead that an organization is prepared to carry.

However, a real problem comes when human resources are cut. Public relations is a relationship-driven activity and relationships are created by and between people. By cutting human resources the ability of public relations to do its job is severely threatened. When times are tight, every other avenue for cost cutting must be explored before cutting people. This is a battle that is sometimes hard to win because it is usually the human resource costs that are the greatest in a public relations department. A simple comparison with advertising illustrates the point. An advertising department may have a staff bill of £100,000, but spend £1,000,000 on media. If cuts come their way, it could be possible to cut the media bills by, say, £100,000 without causing irreparable harm. The public relations department may also have a staff bill of £100,000, but its operating costs could be very low because the programme focuses on media relations, internet-based activities and a face-to-face-based internal communications programme. Costs might be £50,000 or less.

Costs might be saved by trimming the operating budget by the same percentage as the advertising/media cost budget, but 10 per cent of £50,000 is just £5,000. The obvious 'solution' is to cut the human resources where substantial savings can be made. This could spell disaster. Journalists' reasonable expectations might not be met, internet publics may be ignored and the internal communications programme may be reduced. Overall the reputation of the organization will suffer, relationships will be damaged and it may take years to recover.

Human resource costs are linked to the number of people on the programme and the time they spend on it. This is a reasonably simple calculation for in-house departments, but is rather more complicated for consultancy human resources – see later in this chapter. Human resource costs are usually given in terms of hours for the tasks or in person days. So, for an in-house person their total employment costs are taken, the number of days worked per year are calculated (minus weekends and, in some organizations, holidays) and the salary is divided by the number of working days to give a day rate. Hence the cost of an individual day rate may be:

	£
Salary	50,000
Other employment costs (pensions etc)	10,000
	60,000

Days in the year	365
Minus weekends	104
Minus holidays	25
Minus statutory holidays	8
Working days	228

Day rate = 60,000
÷ 228 = £263

Operating or materials costs

These kinds of costs are those items that are associated with delivering the programme, for example, media pack, banners, merchandise, cost of room hire, incentives for filling in questionnaire, cost of advertising space on a website, etc.

When costing out public relations activities two key things need to be borne in mind: effectiveness and efficiency.

The right techniques need to be selected in order for a programme to be effective. When the techniques have been chosen it is then incumbent on the public relations professional to be as efficient as possible. So, for example, it might be decided that an effective way to communicate with important customers is via a magazine. Then choices have to be made on such things as format, number of pages, weight of paper and colour content. There is no need to produce a full-colour magazine just because it looks good. If the content and the right tone can be set by producing a two-colour magazine, then that should be the choice. Against that position, it might be argued that competitors send out colour material and that the organization can't afford to look cheap by comparison. Similarly, if the publication is to be mailed out, the weight of paper will be critical since that, combined with the number of pages, will determine postage costs. Efficient use of resources is important not only from a management point of view, but it may also enable the planner to undertake additional activities within the same overall budget.

The above examples are fairly straightforward. There are other types of decisions that are less easy and are part of the effectiveness debate. Take, for example, a media relations campaign. E-mailings of press releases are relatively cheap, but they are of variable effect. Face-to-face interviews can be extremely effective, but are very costly in terms of time and a very limited number of people can be reached. Somewhere in between there are highly targeted communications, tailor-made to discrete sectors of the press. The same questions of effectiveness and efficiency have to be asked, and the answer will vary depending on the importance of the message and the public being addressed.

Two vital questions need to be asked when looking at effectiveness and efficiency.

Can what is wanted be achieved by spending less money?

By thinking laterally it may be possible to achieve exactly the same objective for a fraction of the cost. Examples of this are use of piggy-back mailings. For instance, building societies and banks post out statements to customers, an ideal opportunity to include additional material.

How about joint ventures with complementary organizations or products? The washing machine and washing powder link-ups are very familiar. It may be possible to sponsor an activity that will opportunities to raise name awareness or undertake corporate hospitality at a fraction of the cost of putting on alternative activities that are totally funded by the organization.

At the other end of the spectrum is the other question on effectiveness.

Will spending a little more add a great deal of value?

Effectiveness does not mean looking to spend the least amount of money all the time; it means getting the most from the money available. Sometimes, by spending a little more, a great deal of value can be added. Take a customer magazine. It could also be mailed out to selected press, to shareholders, to the company pensioners, just for the cost of a run-on of the print plus postage. The effect could be worth many times the extra cost.

It could be that holding an investor briefing on site and getting them all there might be costly, but it could be very effective in tying them more securely to the business both rationally and emotionally.

Equipment

It goes without saying that a programme or campaign cannot run effectively unless there is the right sort of equipment to support it. Public relations professionals do not require vast amounts of equipment, but it is important that it is up to date. Communication professionals need access to, and use of, technology appropriate to their needs. Video conferencing, mobile technology, cameras, access to printers, etc are necessary to do the job.

A note of caution should be sounded. When working on or with international programmes it is easy to assume that every country has ready access to new technologies. This is not the case. It is important therefore not to become wholly dependent on new technology. A fax machine may seem rather dated, but it might be vital.

In summary, when drawing together a budget these three factors must be borne in mind. An example of the main budget headings for a public relations programme is given below.

Budget headings

Human	Operating and materials costs	Equipment
Staff salaries Employment costs (eg NI, pensions, benefits)	Print and production Photography Media relations Conferences, Seminars Sponsorship, etc Operating expenses (eg telephone, stationery, post, travel, subsistence) Overheads and expenses (eg heat, light, office space)	Office furniture Computer equipment and consumables Telephones, cameras special software etc

Working with consultancies

The costs given above are basically the same whether working in-house or in a consultancy. However, when employing consultancies the fees element is obviously different. Fees are payable for the programme agreed upon.

These fees can be negotiated in several ways.

Retainer fee

This covers an agreed amount of consultancy advice, attending meetings, preparing reports, etc. This is usually based on a fixed amount of time per month and the cost will depend on the seniority of the consultant involved. Consultancies like retainers because it guarantees a level of monthly income. Clients like retainers because they have access to expertise on an ongoing basis and often the fee can be negotiated down from a standard hourly rate.

Project fee

This covers the amount of executive time required to implement an agreed programme or campaign. The rate for the project is fixed before it is undertaken and therefore the client can budget precisely what the costs will be. However, if the client brief is not complete, the consultancy will bill for additional items, so skill is required in procuring project work.

Hourly fees plus costs

This covers the actual amount of time spent on the project with time being charged at a pre-agreed rate. The hourly rate will vary depending on the level of expertise needed. The consultancy will also add the costs of materials and expenses and sometimes they add a mark-up on bought-in items (see later). Hourly fees can be an effective way of using consultancies if the task is well scoped. However, if it isn't, large bills can be forthcoming: crisis management assistance is often charged on an hourly rate given that it is difficult to scope this kind of work.

Payment by results

This is an increasingly popular way of billing consultancies. They will be paid on the basis of achieving the results that have been agreed. Often these results are *outputs*, such as number of press comments placed, number of people attending an event and so on. It is a brave consultancy that will be tied to specific *outcomes*, such as X per cent will change their behaviour, since there are so many unknown variables at play.

A number of organizations use a mixture of these ways to procure consultancy advice depending on the nature of advice and support they need.

Consultancies will often charge a 'mark-up' on bought-in services such as photography and print where the consultancy has a legal and financial responsibility for client work (the UK Public Relations Consultants Association (PRCA) recommends 17.65 per cent to cover things like indemnity insurance). Procurers will usually have to pay value added tax (VAT) unless the consultancy is very small and not registered.

A typical monthly invoice from a consultancy might look as follows:

Invoice Headings

	£
Executive time (35 hours at £100 per hour)	3,500.00
Photography (for product launch)	1,200.00
Photography (for in-house magazine)	875.00
Design and print for magazine	3,050.00
Design and print for schools pack	5,750.00
Operating expenses (phone, stationery, post)	350.00
Travel (day return to London and subsistence)	114.50
	14,839.50
VAT at 17.5%	2,596.91
	17,436.41

Overall budgets will be the subject of negotiation. There are, however, a number of approaches to budgeting. The first is to adopt a formula approach that applies company-wide so as to determine the proportion of resources allocated to each function. Typical formulae that are applied are a percentage of the organization's profits or sales turnover, the same as last year or a fixed increase on the previous year's budget, or a sum comparable to that of the closest competitor. The main problem with these approaches is that they take no real account of the actual job of work that is required from public relations. The year ahead may involve a great deal of public relations input, for example if the organization is to mount a major re-branding campaign. The range of publics to be contacted varies from organization to organization, from year to year and from campaign to campaign. For some organizations, public relations as opposed to other forms of marketing communication may be the largest or even the only means of communicative activity.

An alternative approach is to start with the objectives that public relations needs to achieve, cost the tactics required to deliver them, and negotiate the budget on the basis of what is required. This does not give carte blanche to the public relations professional, since it is likely that each activity will be carefully scrutinized and will need to be justified. Wherever possible a cost:benefit analysis should be provided to support public relations expenditure. This entails listing the costs of an activity on one side against the benefits obtained on the other. If a monetary value can be put against these benefits and they outweigh the costs, so much the better. If the benefits include or are largely non-monetary, then the case for funding must be argued on the basis of reputational or relational benefits or the costs associated with these elements not being undertaken. It is also worth doing a reverse analysis and listing the negative costs of not undertaking the activity.

In most instances a mix of formula and costed approaches is taken. Generally speaking an initial indication of the overall budget available will be given, the practitioner will then put together a detailed plan with costings attached, and the final budget will be negotiated. Inevitably compromises will have to be made; however, carefully detailed plans will demonstrate the consequences or risks to which the organization will be exposed if programmes are cut or indicate a list of essential core activities, as well as itemizing the benefits of the full programme.

9

Knowing what has been achieved: evaluation and review

MEASURING SUCCESS

Public relations is no different from any other business function in that it has to demonstrate that it adds value to the organization. Practitioners need to know how effective they've been in meeting their objectives and if they've not been as effective as they thought they should have been, they need to discover why. They also need to be able to demonstrate an appropriate return for the investment that has been made.

First, defining terms. **Evaluation** is an ongoing process when talking about long-term programmes. Thus, there will be regular evaluation of the performance of the website by making a monthly critical analysis of activity. As a result of this there may more focused effort on particular sections of the website, or its navigability features.

Similarly, at the end of a specific campaign, there will be an evolution of the results. So if the objective was to prevent the closure of a factory, there will be a clear-cut indication of the result at the end. The organization has either succeeded or failed. If the objective was to raise awareness by a fixed percentage, then awareness will need to be researched to come to conclusions about levels of success.

Review is a regular management practice. It is extremely sensible to take a good, hard look at the programme each year. Review involves looking at what the evaluation over the year has shown, revisiting the programme objectives and scrutinizing the strategy. The circumstances surrounding the project will also be looked at. Have there been changes that now render it irrelevant, even though evaluation shows it is very successful in itself? It could well be that the project proceeds as before, but it may be that a complete reorientation of the programme is needed. More on this later.

In a nutshell, evaluation is both monitoring as the project proceeds and an analysis of the end results of a campaign or programme, while review is a periodic step back to identify any strategic changes that need to take place.

THE BENEFITS OF EVALUATION

If undertaken properly, evaluation helps spot danger signs before real problems develop and it helps prove the campaigns' worth. Here are a few reasons why evaluation should be built into campaigns and programmes:

- *It focuses effort.* If is is known that the campaign is going to be measured on a number of agreed objectives, it will be focused on the important and keep the urgent in perspective.
- *It demonstrates effectiveness.* There is no success like success! If the practitioners achieves what they have aimed to achieve, they are able to demonstrate their contribution to the organization.
- *It ensures cost efficiency.* Because the things that should take priority are being concentrated on, the budget and time (which is also money) will be spent on the things that count and achieve the big results.
- *It encourages good management.* Management by objectives, having clear goals, brings sharpness to the whole public relations operation. The irrelevant will be quickly identified and rejected.
- *It facilitates accountability.* Not only the practitioners accountability to produce results, which is perfectly in order, but it also makes other people accountable in their dealings. The public relations professional can quite legitimately say, 'If I spend time doing this unscheduled project, it means that I cannot complete this important, planned activity. Which is it to be?' Then clear choices can be made about what may be

new and pressing priorities. If the planned activity is also essential, then extra help may be needed – so the practitioner is in a powerful position to ask for more people or extra budget. Good managers not only accept accountability for themselves, but they are in a strong position to challenge others for access to valued resources.

WHY PRACTITIONERS DON'T EVALUATE

In their book on evaluation for this series, Watson and Noble[1] conclude that many practitioners lack confidence in promoting evaluation methods to clients and employees.

When questioned about their motives for undertaking evaluation, 'prove value of campaign/budget' came out a very clear leader, followed by 'help campaign targeting and planning' and 'need to judge campaign effects'. Another reason, 'help get more resources/fees', came a distant fourth.

Watson's own research showed that practitioners were defensive about their activities. They used evaluation techniques to present data on which they could be judged rather than using evaluation to improve programmes.

The most used technique was providing an output measure for media relations (eg the range of publications in which coverage was obtained) rather than measuring the impact of the media relations campaign itself. Generally speaking, output measurement was seen to be more relevant than gauging impact or gaining intelligence so that programmes could be improved.

Watson also pinpointed the main reasons why programmes were not formally evaluated. These were, first, lack of knowledge (possibly disinclination to learn about evaluation techniques), second, 'cost', followed by 'lack of time' and 'lack of budget'. When added together, 'cost' and 'lack of budget' became the dominant reasons.

There are other reasons why evaluation is seen to be problematic.

- *Understanding what it is that has to be evaluated.* The levels at which evaluation takes place will be discussed later in this chapter, but at this stage suffice to say that often what is measured is output not outcome. There is still an emphasis on media relations and the size of the clippings file. There may be some more sophisticated form of analysis like trying to measure the worth of a clipping depending on its position on the page, its size, the number of key messages it contains and so on. There are several companies that provide such a service. Some will provide a more detailed analysis, for example, a breakdown of how many times specific publications or journalists used press stories and the types of treatment the story received.

However, in the long run it doesn't matter how heavy the clippings file is what matters is what those clippings achieved (the outcome). As a result was there a 20 per cent increase in attendance at the AGM and did they vote in favour of the motion? Has the attitude of key publics altered?

- *Understanding what can be achieved.* Public relations practitioners need to make sober assessments on this. It is just not possible to get the chief executive on the front page of the *Financial Times* every month unless he or she or the organization is exceptional in some way (or notorious!). What is required is an honest appraisal of what can be achieved. That knowledge comes with good research and the benefit of experience. Managing expectations is a key practitioner task.

  Unrealistic expectations on what can be achieved belies a lack of knowledge of the psychological art of the possible. As detailed in Chapter 5 it is very difficult, or at least will require a very determined and skilful campaign, to convert people who have a fixed view to take on the opposite view. It is a less onerous task if the target public has no view at all, or it is reasonably well disposed because the organizational message confirms or aligns with its own desires or views. Again research will identify attitudes and therefore the size of the public relations task.

- *Aggregation.* Sometimes it is difficult to identify precisely what the public relations' contribution was if there were other forms of communication activity, such as special promotions or favourable comment in a social network.

- *Range of evaluation techniques required.* Public relations is unlike some other forms of marketing communication, such as direct mail, where the evaluation is relatively simple: the number of returns and the business transacted. Public relations addresses many audiences in many different ways and different types of evaluation technique are needed. So practitioners need to be aware of the different research techniques available and to have the knowledge and resources necessary to undertake them.

  More recently there have been a number of positive developments that have moved the evaluation agenda along and there are useful guides and books on the subject, such as the CIPR[2] evaluation policy document, the German Public Relations Association[3] online resource on evaluation and, the most comprehensive, the American Institute for Public Relations resources[4]. The book by Dr Tom Watson and Paul Noble in this series provides a comprehensive and practical overview of evaluation. These contributions have helped to take some of the mystique and fear out of the subject.

  It is impossible in this book to give an evaluation blueprint for every type of public relations activity. For some activities evaluation will be relatively easy. If a practitioner is running an exhibition stand it is a simple, quantitative exercise to count the number of product enquiries, take contact addresses and then trace back subsequent product orders.

Other things like the effects of a long-term sponsorship programme are much more difficult to evaluate.

PRINCIPLES OF EVALUATION

There are a number of principles of evaluation that help to set the context and make the task easier.

- *Objectives* are critical. Public relations campaigns can be seen to be effective when they achieve their objectives in a well-managed way. So objectives need to be achievable and measurable and, to ensure that they are, it needs research and pre-testing wherever possible. 'Raising awareness' is not a good objective unless qualified by how much (1 per cent or 99 per cent?) and with whom (define the public). Research will help to show you what is possible. There is also likely to be a timeframe over which to work. A long-term campaign to change the general attitude towards the decriminalization of drugs is likely to have patchy, incremental results over a long period. However, even in this situation it is possible to lay down clear benchmarks. For example, a legitimate objective would be to persuade the majority of chief con-stables by the year 2012, or give up the campaign.

  The achievement of objectives is the clearest way to evaluate any programme or campaign. Hence, it is also imperative that these and the measurement criteria that will be used to assess them are agreed with those who will judge success.
- *Evaluation* needs to be considered at the beginning of the process. It's too late to ask the question 'How did we do?' at the end if the practitioner didn't build in the mechanisms for measurement at the beginning.
- *Evaluation* is ongoing. Programmes should be monitored as they progress and initial findings scrutinized to judge both whether the indicators point to success, and to fine-tune the programme where adjustments need to be made.
- *Evaluation* is at all stages of the communication process. The decisions that have to be taken all along the communication chain affect the communication outcome. Practitioners have to decide on the content, the tone, the medium, the level of exposure, whether the target is receiving and interpreting the communication correctly. If one element is wrong, the desired outcome will be in jeopardy. Unfortunately, the converse is not true. Just because each element is right doesn't mean automatic success, but getting any of the elements wrong diminishes the chances of success.

- *Evaluation* must be as objective and scientific as possible. This means that public relations practitioners need to be proficient themselves or need to enlist the services of specialists who know about social scientific research and evaluation methods. Sometimes less rigorous research gives an indicator, but evaluation must be valid and demonstrably reliable if it is to be taken seriously.
- *Evaluating* programmes and processes. Public relations programmes and campaigns require evaluating for the results of the communication activity, and also for their management. It is useful to separate out and list the achievements of programme objectives (eg sponsorship achieved objective of 20 per cent awareness in target group) and the fact that the campaign was managed well (eg 10 per cent under budget).

EVALUATION TERMINOLOGY

There are a number of terms that are often used in evaluation that merit explanation. For each programme or campaign there will be:

- *Input.* This is what the public relations professional 'puts in' to their communication 'products'. For example, they might write, design and produce an in-house journal. When evaluating inputs, elements such as the quality of the background research, writing, effectiveness of design, choice of font and size, paper and colour can all be evaluated.
- *Output.* This is how effectively 'products' are distributed to and used by the target publics, either by the target public directly (eg how many employees received and read the journal) or by a third party who is a channel or opinion former to the target public (eg how many bloggers used the key messages?). So evaluation of outputs often involves counting and analysing things, for example, readership and circulation, reach of websites and content analysis.
- *Out-take.* This is the intermediate position between an output and an outcome, and describes what an individual might extract from a communications programme, but it may or may not lead to further action that can be measured as a result. If a message in the house magazine is about discounted membership of the local cinema club, how many employees actually remember that message can be measured, ie have extracted the relevant information from the article, but there is likely to be a difference between the number who demonstrate an out-take from the magazine and those who go on to sign up for membership.
- *Outcome.* This involves measuring the end effect of the communication. How many employees who read the magazine took up the opportunity

to join the local cinema club at a reduced rate? Outcomes are measured at the three levels at which objectives are set:

- changes at the thinking or awareness level (cognitive);
- changes in the attitude or opinion level (affective);
- changes in behaviour (conative).

To measure these outcomes sometimes requires sophisticated research, including attitude surveys, focus groups, tracking web or social networking traffic and content and individual interviews. For some campaigns, however, measurement can be relatively easy, for example as sales at the launch of a product.

Thus it can be seen that if changes in opinion are wanted as the result of the campaign, this will be the objective, and to evaluate the programme opinions will need to be measured. It is not good enough to show newspaper cuttings that contain the message practitioners wish to get across in order to change opinions. Media relations is a route by which the end may be achieved, and success in this area is worth noting, but it is not the end result. Success in the media is an output, not an outcome.

Measuring success at the output level and claiming that by implication an outcome has been achieved is called 'level substitution' and is invalid. Of course it is perfectly legitimate to measure outputs as an indicator along the way, but that is how they must be described.

Outflow

This is the long-term cumulative effects of public relations in terms of individual programmes, or the aggregated effect of several campaigns and programmes. Hence, this may be, for example, improvement of the reputation of the organization as a result of numerous campaigns over time; or it might be a long-term change in one particular behaviour as a result of several campaigns, or one long campaign that comprises several stages each with their own outcomes, but whose cumulative effect is more than the aggregate of those campaigns. For example, smoking is decreasing in the Western World, but that is the result of many different campaigns over several years and the gradual change in public opinion that has now made it less socially acceptable.

The results from the European Communication Monitor for 2009[5] showed that most practitioners still measure at the level of output, with 84 per cent relying on monitoring media clippings and responses and 64 per cent monitoring internet/intranet usage. Only just over half (54 per cent) measured outcomes.

LEVELS OF EVALUATION

Chapter 1 described the contribution of public relations at four levels: societal, management, programme (which includes programmes and campaigns) and individual activities. In a similar vein, evaluation can be undertaken at these various levels. Gregory and White[6] provide a detailed explanation of some activities, but it is clear that at the societal level, apart from the societal contribution that organizations can make, public relations can have a role to play in bringing to the public agenda things that are significant for the whole of society, such as, for example, explaining and convincing people of the need for action over climate change. It can also bring to public notice the concerns of minority groups who might otherwise lack the power to claim attention. Hence, the plight of elderly people who find difficulty in paying their fuel bills can be highlighted by activist groups who use public relations very effectively. Public relations can be involved in bringing together groups who are in conflict, as in Northern Ireland, with profound positive social effect.

As Gregory and White explain, or organizations, public relations at the societal level can be used, for example to promote a social responsibility agenda and be the eyes and ears of the organization, helping it to adapt to changes in the social environment.

Evaluation of the impact of public relations activity at the societal level requires tools that will measure things such as public opinion: hence public opinion polling by the interested organization, whether that be government or a corporate body, or by one of the larger opinion survey organizations, such as Ipsos MORI, will provide feedback. Other tools such as mass observation of behaviour and large quantitative and qualitative surveys are also relevant here. At this level, as for the other three levels, awareness, attitude and opinion and behaviour towards the organization will need to be evaluated.

At the management level, public relations will make a contribution to the overall reputation of the organization, ensuring management decisions are informed. Thus it may also contribute directly to profits. Being the guardian of the organization's reputation and safeguarding the quality of key relationships with stakeholders will be invaluable. Profit is a tangible asset that can be added to the balance sheet, but reputation and the quality of relationships form part of the intangible assets of the organization and are not immediately amenable to a financial measure. However, when the organization comes to be sold, these intangible assets begin to realize their true value. Organizations that are taken over are often paid more for the value of their brand (that is, their reputation and the relationship people have with the brand) than for the tangible assets (buildings, money, equipment, etc). Hence, organizations now often use the balanced scorecard approach to judge their worth. Balanced scorecards attempt to evaluate both the

163

tangible and intangible assets of an organization and therefore provide a fuller picture of its value than a summation of its financial worth alone. Figure 9.1 gives an example of how such a scorecard can be adapted to evaluate public relations' contribution at the corporate level, along with two example questions that might be asked under each heading.

Financial	Reputational
• Did our financial PR efforts increase share value? • Did PR contribute to product sales?	• Is the organization held in higher esteem than it was 5 years ago? • Do more people see us as an employer of choice?
Relational	Political
• Do our corporate stakeholders trust us more now than 5 years ago? • Do our partnerships last longer than they did 5 years ago?	• Do more MPs and government officials know of and support our organization than 5 years ago? • Are we more effective in our lobbying campaigns than 5 years ago?

Figure 9.1 *A Balanced Scorecard approach to evaluating corporate-level public relations performance*

To evaluate at this level there will have to be in-depth qualitative and quantitative research using techniques such as: focus groups, one-to-one interviews, opinion surveys, online discussion groups, online opinion sampling and organizational profiling, in-house questionnaires and surveys, analysis of sales returns and so on.

At the programme level much more detailed work has been done on producing evaluation models.

A PROGRAMME EVALUATION MODEL AND SOME OTHER MEASURES

It is possible to come up with an evaluation model that can be applied to most programmes, but there is no gold standard for evaluation – individual programmes and campaigns need tailor-made evaluations.

A useful device widely used today is the macro model of evaluation devised by Jim Macnamara[7] (see Figure 9.2). The model forms a pyramid.

At the base are inputs, basically information and planning, and at the peak, objectives achieved. Each activity is split down into the various steps of the communication process. At the input stage the model asks the user to make a judgement on the quality of information, the choice of medium and the content of the communication. It then considers outputs, that is the communication produced, for example, the newsletter, the press release, the brochure, the website. It goes on to look at out-take, that is, what receivers have paid attention to and retained, and then it considers the results or outcomes – what the communication actually achieved. Alongside the steps is a list of evaluation methods that might be used for a media campaign, a newsletter, a website and so on.

The model needs to be customized for each project, but the principles remain the same. Its strength is that it recognizes a range of evaluation methods and allows flexibility.

The more advanced evaluation methods further up the pyramid measure outcomes. They are more sophisticated and of course more expensive. The ones lower down the pyramid are more basic and can be seen as tests that things are being done right, more akin to quality control. However, these basic checks are not to be missed. There can be more confidence of success higher up the pyramid if the basics are right.

In practical terms how does this translate into reality? Here is a resume checklist of critical factors to consider when planning evaluation into a campaign or programme:

- set measurable objectives;
- build in evaluation and quality checks from the start;
- agree measurement criteria with whoever will be judging the success of your work;
- establish monitoring procedures that are open and transparent, for example, monthly reviews of progress;
- demonstrate results.

As mentioned earlier in this book (Chapter 5) communication is not only about rational engagement; the emotions also play a significant role. While the author would always recommend evaluation to be scientifically evaluated, it is true that subjective as well as objective measures are made.

Objective evaluation measures

Typical objective measures that might be employed are:

- changes in behaviour (if a product is given public relations support, buyer behaviour can be tracked);

Evaluation of public relations programme

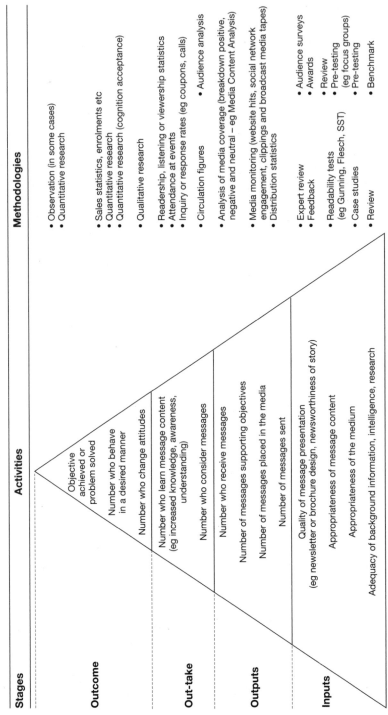

Stages	Activities	Methodologies
Outcome	Objective achieved or problem solved	• Observation (in some cases) • Quantitative research
	Number who behave in a desired manner	• Sales statistics, enrolments etc • Quantitative research • Quantitative research (cognition acceptance)
	Number who change attitudes	• Qualitative research
	Number who learn message content (eg increased knowledge, awareness, understanding)	• Readership, listening or viewership statistics • Attendance at events • Inquiry or response rates (eg coupons, calls)
Out-take	Number who consider messages	• Circulation figures • Audience analysis
	Number who receive messages	• Analysis of media coverage (breakdown positive, negative and neutral – eg Media Content Analysis)
	Number of messages supporting objectives	
Outputs	Number of messages placed in the media	• Media monitoring (website hits, social network engagement, clippings and broadcast media tapes) • Distribution statistics
	Number of messages sent	
	Quality of message presentation (eg newsletter or brochure design, newsworthiness of story)	• Expert review • Feedback • Awards • Audience surveys
Inputs	Appropriateness of message content	• Readability tests (eg Gunning, Flesch, SST) • Review • Pre-testing (eg focus groups)
	Appropriateness of the medium	• Case studies • Pre-testing
	Adequacy of background information, intelligence, research	• Review • Benchmark

Figure 9.2 *Macnamara's macro model of evaluation adapted by Gregory*

- responses (return of reply-paids, response slips, salesforce quotes, etc);
- changes in attitude, opinion and awareness – especially important for opinion-former work (can be measured through telephone research, questionnaires, one-to-one interviews, online surveys);
- achievements (80 per cent of retailers came to promotional conference);
- media coverage, content, distribution, readership, share of voice (content analysis, readership data);
- budget control and value for money (a process measure).

It is sometimes relatively easy to put in checks when measuring the effectiveness of editorial when working on a product promotion programme, if working in conjunction with other marketing colleagues. For example, when the author worked in-house for a large building society, she was able to place editorial material next to a financial product advert that had been running for a few weeks in the *Sunday Times*. The number of policies that came from the two adverts previous to the editorial were 27 and 21 respectively. The advert with adjacent editorial resulted in 94 policies being sold from coupons.

Similarly, for another financial product it was found that adjacent editorial doubled the coupon returns from a series of adverts in the *Sunday Telegraph*.

Subjective evaluation measures

Apart from quantitative objective measures, subjective measures of performance are also inevitably employed. Public relations is a human business and human judgements will be used. These factors may be especially important in the client/consultancy relationship, but are also highly prized in the relationships that in-house departments build with other departments within their organization. In fact what often wins business for consultancies (all things being equal) and ready co-operation from other departments are these subjective yardsticks:

- enthusiasm;
- efficiency and professionalism;
- creativity;
- initiative;
- an instinct for what is right in a given situation (based on judgement gained through experience);
- people chemistry.

Evaluating the process

A critical part of evaluation is to monitor the process. Part of this is the effective deployment of both staff and budgets. Regular, rigorous monitoring of both is required.

Staff need to be continuously developed to cope with and exploit the rapidly changing communication environment. It is also essential that public relations staff are well motivated and well directed. They are, after all, the handlers and managers of the organization's reputation in a most overt sense. If they do not believe in what they are doing, how can they do their job proficiently and professionally?

Likewise, the management and effective use of budgets is a duty laid on every manager, including the public relations professional. With so many options open on how to spend what is often quite a limited budget, he or she must have a keen regard to the careful stewardship of resources. Every pound should count. Chapter 8 gives a more detailed exposition on how budgeting can be done effectively.

The Olympic Bid Case Study

This case study shows how research and evaluation is embedded throughout a planned campaign and demonstrates research and evaluation at the four levels described in Chapter 4: formative, programme, monitoring and evaluative.

How ongoing evaluation helped The UK Olympic bid

Since the inception of the modern Olympic movement in 1894, Britain has been a major participant, playing host to the Games in 1908 and 1948, and sending hundreds of Olympians to compete. In subsequent years, Britain made two unsuccessful bids, but London was nominated as an official candidate city for the 2012 Games in May 2004. It then had to put together a compelling case for London to host the Games in what Mike Lee, Director of Communications for the London 2012 Olympic bid, called the 'most competitive ever bidding procedure mounted by the International Olympics Committee'. The task was to convince the 117 International Olympics Committee (IOC) members that London could deliver on five selection criteria:

- the best Olympic plan;
- low-risk delivery;
- an enthusiastic country;
- clear benefits of the Games in London;
- a professional, likeable and trustworthy team.

This case concentrates on the research and evaluation activities for the communication targeted at the British public, especially in London. The aim of the communication was around the third selection criterion; demonstrating an enthusiastic country.

There were two main objectives:

- building and maintaining levels of support (attitudinal);
- driving registration of a 'vote' of support (behavioural).

It was recognized that achieving the first objective was a prerequisite for achieving the second.

A number of sub-objectives, in support of the two main objectives given above, were identified:

- engender a sense of pride around the London bid;
- specify the need to register a vote of support (via texting, e-mail, etc);
- build knowledge around the benefits of London hosting the bid;
- inspire confidence that London could win the bid.

Formative benchmarking research done by the 2012 Olympic bid organization, using polls and qualitative focus groups, identified themes that would resonate with the public, and national pride came to the fore. Given that enthusiasm was the selection criteria that the IOC were to use in their final judgements, support was identified as the measure of success, for both main objectives, with the key questions, 'Would you like London to be chosen as host city of the 2012 Olympic Games?' and 'Will you, or have you, registered your support?'. To underpin this, the 2012 organization kept a database tracking the number of people registering their support.

The promotional budget was limited so the two main communication channels were poster and billboard advertising using donated space around London's public transport hubs, complemented by media relations and some limited and donated TV advertising. An overarching theme 'Make Britain Proud' became the strap-line for the advertising and was a core media message.

In November 2004, Ipsos-MORI undertook a poll on behalf of the IOC to judge initial support for the bid. The result was that public support was in the high sixties – an acceptable level, and influential in London going forward as a candidate city.

i to i research was recruited at the beginning of 2005 in the lead up to the IOC decision to measure the effectiveness of the communications. They identified two core issues, first that persuasive messages lose their impact over time and enthusiasm had to be maintained between the time when London was announced as a candidate city and the vote of the IOC members a year later. Second, the London bid would inevitably attract negative publicity on things such as cost, disruption, poor legacy, etc and i to i research needed to advise on the impact of this negativity on the general public.

Research was therefore needed to:

- anticipate any wavering support and 'weak spots' for the bid (formative and programme research);
- provide insight into how well the communication was helping to maintain support levels, build voter registration and deliver key messages (programme and monitoring);
- determine how well the campaign delivered the aims of the 2012 organization (evaluative).

i to i research conducted two waves of research: in January 2005, to coincide with the IOC visit to London, and in May 2005, before the announcement of the bid results in July of 2005. Online surveys and content analysis of media were the main research tools.

Wave 1 provided an indication of how well support levels were holding up (formative research), given that there would be a dip after the initial euphoria of London being declared a candidate city. The results would also inform the development of the communication plan (programme).

The results showed that the reach and frequency of the communication was good. For the advertising it was estimated that almost all Londoners had a chance to see the posters and limited TV advertising at least 10 times, and 98 per cent of Londoners recalled either advertising or public relations activity. A third recalled the pride message. Content analysis of the media relations activity was undertaken to make a judgement on what messages Londoners were likely to be taking from the coverage and how positively or negatively they felt about the coverage. Media messages sought to support the four sub-objectives given earlier. The analysis of the print media showed a high volume of articles referencing the benefits of the Games, but this was being diluted by stories about the potential cost to Londoners. Furthermore, despite good recall of the advertising and public relation messages on pride and a need to support the bid, only 7 per cent mentioned the need for people to register their support by way of a petition vote. The research also revealed that 59 per cent of Londoners claimed to have had a discussion with a colleague, friend or family member about the bid, which demonstrated the power of word of mouth, but it was concerning that a third of these conversations were negative.

To address the issue of wavering support and weak spots, Wave 1 of the research identified that:

- Advertising was engendering a general feeling of national pride and support, but not communicating the need for, and importance of people registering their support.
- Public relations activity was filling the gaps in communicating the benefits. However, reporting of the negatives was diluting the benefits.
- Those seeing advertising only, were more negative than any other group.

A hypothesis was formed that, although messages about the benefits were getting through, there might be a group of people who were unsupportive of the bid and 'infecting' others with their opinions.

To research the second issue, which was to identify where the support was strongest and weakest, Londoners were segmented using two axes; engagement in sport, and attitudes towards Britain hosting events in general. For the first axis a battery of attitudinal statements was used to gauge interest and participation in sport, and for the other axis, a battery of statements around the United Kingdom hosting events in general. The results segmented Londoners into four categories as shown in Figure 9.3.

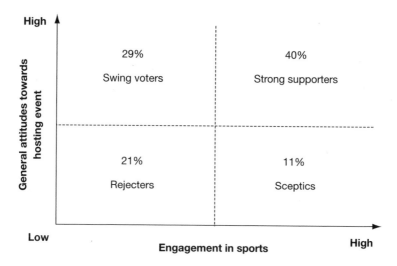

Figure 9.3 *Segmentation of support*

Strong supporters ranked high on both measures, whilst Rejecters ranked low on both measures. The two groups who showed the weakest support for the Games – the Sceptics and the Rejecters – were sizeable and negative on two aspects of the bid: confidence in the government to spend money effectively (cost had earlier shown as an issue of concern), and sense of pride about London as a host of the Games. A high concentration of Rejecters and Sceptics had seen only the advertising, they were more negative and had a higher propensity to breed negativity through word of mouth. The concern was, therefore, at this stage of the campaign (January 2005), that the 29 per cent of Londoners who were Swing Voters could be 'infected' and influenced by the negative opinions of Sceptics and Rejecters. This could have an adverse effect on support and could have slowed registration. Furthermore, it was found that older people and women were more likely to be Rejecters as they are less involved in sports and more likely to have concerns about costs.

It was clear then that the communication had to be adjusted (programme and monitoring research). Effort needed to be put in to shore-up support from the Swing Voters and the number of people registering their support for London's bid had to be increased. Given constraints on budget and the long lead times for poster media, public relations was the principal vehicle for an intensified campaign getting across the benefits of hosting the Games, such as improved facilities and transport, and the importance of registering support.

The Wave 2 research undertaken in May measured the success of the refocused campaign. By supplying media with positive stories, negativity was drowned out and support among the Waverers increased between January and May 2005 – up from 36 per cent to 52 per cent among the Swing Voters and from 31 per cent to 53 per cent among the Sceptics. The IOC visit to London in February provided an ideal opportunity to showcase to both them and Londoners in general that London was the ideal

171

Olympic choice. By May 63 per cent of Londoners were able to cite something positive about the bid, a considerable increase from February.

Another weakness in the earlier communication had been identified; people did not understand why it was important to register their support for the bid. By May, 67 per cent of Londoners understood that the main purpose of their role was to 'show the IOC that there is public support'. Between February and May, registered support rose by 7 per cent and the 2012 bid organization's own database showed registration rising from 1 million at the beginning of the year, to 3 million by July. The focus on the IOC February visit demonstrated the need to show support and an unintended, but good consequence was a growing belief that London could win the bid. Matching the results to the original sub-objectives (evaluative research), it can be clearly seen that the communication campaign succeeded.

This case clearly demonstrates the benefits that can accrue by using research and evaluation at the four levels indicated in Chapter 4: formative, programme, monitoring and evaluative. The use of research not only ensured that the campaign was well-founded, but it guided the development and adjustment of the campaign as it unfolded and ensured that its impact was focused and clear for all to see. Without the embedding of research at these four levels, the success of the campaign would have been in doubt and it certainly would not have delivered the results that it did.

MEDIA ANALYSIS

Having said that media analysis is a measure of output rather than outcome, it is still very significant as the European Communication Monitor research has shown. So it is vital that media campaigns are seen to be delivering at the output level. The following case study illustrates the point and shows how media evaluation can be part of a wider evaluation programme.

How media evaluation helps the McDonald's business

How does a global brand keep track of the many hundreds of press articles and online comments that are made about it every day? McDonald's is constantly under the spotlight for everything from the quality of its food to its management. All this 'noise' affects the brand and how it is viewed by various stakeholders.

McDonald's opened its first restaurant in the UK in 1974. Today more than 2.5 million people use its services every day.

In January 2006 McDonald's commissioned Echo, an international media analysis and communication research company, to evaluate their media coverage in support of their key business objective, which is to build trust in McDonald's in the UK? Performance against this objective is assessed through year-on-year measurable improvements in:

- media coverage favourability (increase positive and neutral);
- monthly consumer tracking study under the headline measure of trust.

In June 2006, McDonald's Vice President for Communications UK, Nick Hindle, stipulated that Echo's regular report should provide a summary of the brand positioning and details of forward-looking issues. The primary objective of the report was to enable McDonald's to monitor the status of their 'brand health' each month and to identify emerging issues in their industry, as well as forthcoming industry activities or events, that could influence the business or communication strategy and planning. Thus, the key objectives of the project were to:

- design a visually stimulating and informative dashboard style report, which provided a barometer of brand positioning and clear display of critical forward-looking issues;
- produce an appropriate tone and style of reporting for McDonald's Executive Team, which could also be shared with McDonald's European Communication Teams;
- analyse cumulative findings of McDonald's existing stakeholder research, giving insight into opportunities and potential challenges for the brand;
- provide a snapshot of critical industry issues/events arising over the next six months in areas of food, people, sport, media and environment.

A two-page dashboard-style report was developed to illustrate an overview of brand positioning on the front page and a calendar of industry issues/events overleaf.

Key insights and data from Echo's media evaluation and existing McDonald's stakeholder research studies were depicted through graphic illustrations and text highlights. The second-page calendar of forthcoming events was divided into sections on food, people, sport, media and environment, with information on the likely dates, web links and further details of the event organizer provided for each activity listed. Echo also added a 'Red Alerts' section at the top of the second page, to highlight critical future issues that could potentially impact on the McDonald's brand.

Execution/implementation:

Overview of brand positioning

For this section, information was gathered from existing McDonald's stakeholder research studies to display perceptions amongst the media and consumers.

The front page gave strong visual presentation of the top line results of each study, supported by integrated analysis of the research findings, which identified strengths and areas for improvement. As the report was designed for an executive level audience, commentary was intentionally kept to a minimum, to include key insights, emerging trends and any correlations or anomalies across the groups.

Calendar of Industry Events

This required a radical approach, using non-traditional methods of media research. Echo set up a method of identifying emerging issues and forthcoming events, through using a combination of internet research and web spider software programmes that alerted them to any new information on the internet relating to the following:

- food – eg obesity debate, food labelling/nutrition, marketing to children, Ofcom regulation;
- people – employment issues relating to food/retail industry, legislation, best practice, conferences, etc;
- sport – particularly in relation to the London Olympics, sports sponsorship/marketing;
- media – future features on TV/Radio about McDonald's or in the area of food/obesity/topical issues; eg episodes of *You Are What You Eat*, *Newsnight* features, *Chew on This*, *Fast Food Nation* movie; date of film releases/who is releasing them;
- environment – conferences/events in relation to impact of food manufacture and production on the environment; impact of McDonald's on local or global environment.

Echo's approach to integrating media and other forms of evaluation has led to a new style of reporting that is useful not only to the communication team, but to senior executives. Nick Hindle recently described the report as 'the Holy Grail', 'concise', 'adds value' and 'what everybody wants' (objective 1).

The report now forms part of the VP Communications UK's monthly update on business and brand performance to the Executive Team (objective 2). The European Corporate Relations team also receive the report on a monthly basis (objective 2). Additionally, the reports are more widely distributed, going to the Executive Team, Internal Communications Team, External Agencies and Brand Ambassadors (media trained franchisees).

Integrated analysis has helped McDonald's to gain a wider perspective of key brand strengths and stakeholder positioning (objective 3). Echo highlights opportunities and risks each month, identifying where similar and conflicting trends are seen across the stakeholder groups. An example of this is their reputation in the area of Corporate Social Responsibility (CSR), where MPs had negative perceptions, whilst in the media regional community, work was driving strong community message and CSR reputation (Appendix 3). A comprehensive diary of industry issues and events, detecting new information each month, fulfils objective 4.

The ultimate test of any evaluation system is a business tool: it tell you now relationships with key stakeholders are developing. According to Nick Hindle:

> Our dashboard is now part of how we do business at McDonald's. We're all on the same page, using the same language and aware of how well our corporate communication is connecting with our audiences.

REVIEWING THE SITUATION

While monitoring and evaluation takes place on an ongoing basis, a thorough review takes place less often. As explained earlier (Chapter 4), a major review including extensive research may well be triggered by a significant event such as a takeover or a new Chief Executive arriving. That will entail a close examination and analysis of both the external and internal environments, and probably a repositioning of the organization, as well as all the aspects of constructing a viable plan outlined in this book.

All good managers undertake a regular review of their programmes. A look every 3 or 6 months and a longer look every 12 months ensures that everything is on track, and that any new situations are taken into account. Minor modifications can be made as the programme progresses.

The annual review will need to be tough and may involve examining new or ongoing research. A day or couple of days away from the office with colleagues who are working on the programme is time well spent to ensure that all is in order. It is done in addition to the full evaluation at the end of a programme.

While it is essential to tweak tactics as a plan unfolds, especially in the light of information that ongoing evaluation brings, the plan itself should remain as the route-map, with some flexibility to accommodate opportunities and problems as they arise. That is because the objectives remain the same and the strategy holds good. However, it is essential to bear in mind that public relations is conducted within a dynamic environment and there must be the capability to respond as soon as possible, either in a proactive way to lead or forestall events, or in a reactive way to deal with an emergency situation. A review is required if the overall objectives need to be changed or if the strategy is seen not to be working.

The strategy's not working

If the underlying strategy for a programme or campaign turns out to be wrong, this is a very serious business. To get the strategy wrong indicates fundamental flaws in research or the interpretation of research. An example will illustrate. Suppose a company wants to launch a high-quality new product and the public relations strategy is to mount a media relations campaign including a press launch with product demonstrations, merchandising packs for the regional and consumer press, competitions, consumer offers and a couple of stunts designed to attract attention.

Suppose after all this, the product doesn't sell at all well. There are a number of explanations and here are just a few:

- The product is sub-standard. As soon as the public relations professional becomes aware of this the company must be advised accordingly. If the company insists on going ahead, at least it was told. The public relations professional may resign over such an issue. The damage to long-term reputation could be severe.
- The product is a 'me too' and has no distinguishing features. No amount of good public relations will persuade people to buy this type of product

rather than their current favourite, unless of course there are brand strengths. Public relations should not over-promise.

- The product and the contents of the campaign are aimed at the wrong target markets. There is a major flaw in research.
- The content is not being accepted. It could be that the wrong things are being said, or in the wrong way, or that the medium or the timing is wrong. There is lack of research or misinterpretation of information.
- The product needs to be sampled by consumers for them to really appreciate it. Then why choose media relations as the main communication vehicle?
- The press aren't interested. The right media hook has not been identified: they are not being approached in the right way. It could be lack of research. Maybe another big consumer story is breaking at the same time as the launch. Sometimes all the market intelligence and research in the world can't protect from this nightmare. In this case the strategy may even be right, but either that or tactics will have to be changed quickly to get back on the front foot again. Creativity counts.

If the strategy is not working two questions need to be asked:

- *Are the objectives right and realizable?* If the answer to that is 'no' then no matter how brilliant it is the strategy will not work. If the answer is 'yes' then the second question is necessary.
- *What's wrong with the strategy?* What basic points have been overlooked or misinterpreted? This means a return to the research, and a careful analysis. Were the right questions asked in the first place? Were they all asked? What do the unanswered questions really indicate? Is there a clear understanding of publics and what can be achieved? Do the messages have credibility and can they be delivered via the tactics selected? Is the programme too ambitious or perhaps not sufficiently ambitious? Is the programme adequately resourced?

It is embarrassing to say the least to get the strategy wrong but, if careful research has been done and there can be confidence in the interpretation, it is likely that the tactics, not the strategy, needs correcting. However, as with all things, it is better to admit when something is wrong and correct it, rather than limp along wasting time and resources, and damaging professional reputations.

External and internal review drivers

Through the regular evaluation and review process, adjustments will be made to campaigns or programmes. Objectives might be refocused or given a different priority and tactics may be altered. This is part of being effective and in tune with changing requirements. Minor ongoing changes can be expected. However, all the best-laid plans are subject to major review or even reversal if fundamental changes in the external or internal environment call for it. Thankfully these 'drivers' occur relatively infrequently, but it is wise to have contingency plans ready to deal with them if or when they do arise, because they usually require fast-footed action. Careful risk analysis should help in preparing for these eventualities along with an issue management programme.

The list below gives a flavour of the sort of external drivers that could force a review:

- legislative change that either threatens or gives expanded opportunities to the organization;
- competitor activity, which threatens or gives opportunity;
- takeover or acquisition (note, if a company is taken over through a hostile bid it then has to switch its public relations endeavour from actively campaigning against the acquirers to working for them);
- major product recall or damage to corporate reputation;
- action by a well-organized, powerful, opposing pressure group.

Internal drivers can also make a review essential. The kinds of scenarios that would force this are:

- restructure with new priorities, which may entail the splitting up or restructuring of the public relations function;
- changes in key personnel such as the chief executive (or the director of public relations);
- budget changes, meaning that public relations activity is significantly cut or expanded;
- future needs: a programme or campaign may end or run out of steam; a fresh look is then required to reactivate and refocus the public relations work.

Once having decided on a review, the planning process then begins its cycle again. Figure 3.2 on page 40 outlines the process. Again the basic questions have to be addressed:

- What am I trying to achieve?
- Who do I want to reach?
- What do I want to say?
- What are the most effective ways of getting the message across?
- How can success be measured?

By systematically working through these questions, all the essentials of planning and managing a successful public relations programme will be covered.

AND FINALLY

This book has given the basic framework for putting together a well-founded public relations campaign. Careful, systematic planning will make life much easier. Add one more vital ingredient – flair, the ability to think creatively and not be bound by tramlines, and work in public relations will be immensely rewarding. There is nothing more exciting than seeing a communication programme work and take on a life that can only come from the sort of skills the public relations professional can provide. Communication is about making contact, developing relationships, building trust and achieving results which add to the success of the organization because key stakeholders are supportive. Careful planning and management lies at the heart of that.

Notes

1. Watson, T and Noble, P (2007) *Evaluating Public Relations*, Kogan Page, London.
2. Available to CIPR members at www.cipr.co.uk/News/research/evalua tion_June05.pdf.
3. Available at www.communicationcontrolling.de/index/php?id=227 &=3.
4. Available at www.Institutepr.org/research/measurement_and_evalua ation.
5. For more information see www.communicationmonitor.eu.
6. Gregory, A and White, J (2008) Introducing the Chartered Institute of Public Relations work on research and evaluation, in B van Ruler, A Tkalac Vercic and D Vercic (eds) *Public Relations Metrics: research and evaluation*, Routledge, New York.
7. Macnamara, J R (1992) Evaluation of public relations: the Achilles' heel of the PR profession, *International Public Relations Review*, **15**, November.

Index

advertising   122
AIDA model   87
aims   89–90 *see also* objectives
American Institute for Public
    Relations   159
annual report   116
Apple   4
Appleby Horse Fair   84–85
Armani   112
Arthur W Page Society   1
    The Authentic Enterprise   1, 32
Asda   7
    Pulse of Nation research
    7–8
attitudes   77–78, 90–91
    communication and   82, 10
    influences on   77–78
        commonly held beliefs   78
        conditioning   78
        facts   78
    first-hand knowledge   77
    media   78
    second-hand knowledge   78

stakeholder   97
    surveys   162
audience   24

balanced scorecard   163, 164
Beckham, David   112
behaviour   91
    evaluating changes to   167
    influencing   10
blogs   6
BMRB International (British Market
    Research Bureau)   132
brand   163 *see also* reputation
bridge-spanners   84
British Airways   11–12
Broom, Glen   18, 20, 40, 41
budgeting   155
business case   47

campaigns   22 *see also* programmes
case studies
    Guide Dogs for the Blind
        Association (GDBA) 125–27,

Independent Financial Advisors
  promotion 131–34
Love Food, Hate Waste
  69–73
McDonald's case study
  172–74
Olympic Bid 168–72
The Piper's Trail (Army in
  Scotland) 128–31
Sheep Drive Over London
  Bridge 145–49
'Snorers Sleep-in' 74–75
Center, Allen 40, 41
Central Office of Information
  (COI) 121, 124
Chartered Institute of Public
  Relations (CIPR) 3, 159
chief executive, role of 6
coaching 2
cognitive changes 162
communication 1–2
  behaviour, influencing 10
  content 113–14
  'convergence model' 80–81,
    83
  'co-orientation model' 81
  'Domino Theory' 86–87
  evaluation 11–14
  groups and 81–82
  importance of 10–11
  internal 2
  mass audiences 82–85
  mass media 82–85
  network models 83
  objectives 25, 76–96
  publics and 100–03
  proposition 110–11
  Reception Theory 88
  relationships with publics
    11
  skill 9–11
  'two-step' model 82
  Uses and Gratification
    Theory 87–88
  see also internet, message,
    networking, programme
communication chain 78–86
  feedback 79
  model 79
communication manager
  18–19
  communication facilitator 19
  expert prescriber 19
  problem-solving process
    facilitator 19
  see also public relations
    professional
communications audit 59, 68
community relations 123
Computer Aided Telephone
  Interview (CATI) system
  65
conative (acting) objectives 91
  evaluating 162
conferences 123
consultancies (PR) 153–55
  hourly fees 154
  payment by results 154–55
  project fee 153–54
  retainer fee 153
consumerism 55
contingency planning 134–35
  major crises 134
  role of PR professional 135
  scenarios 135
  strategic 135
  tactical 135
corporate identity 122
corporate social responsibility
  (CSR) 61
crisis management 123
Critical Path Analysis (CPA)
  141–43
  examples 142
Cumbria County Council 84–85
customer relationships 5
customers 97
Cutlip, Scott 40, 41

De Santo   21
'deliberative engagement'   110
demographic changes   55
DEMOS   55
Department of Health   27
direct mail   122, 159
'Domino Theory'   86–87
Dozier, David   18, 19, 20

Echo Research   172–74
Edwards, L   12
Einstein, Albert   93
emotional appeals   112–13
   fear   112–13
   guilt   113
   humour   112
   love   112
   sex   112
   virtue   112
employees   5
   social networks   6
environmental context/issues
      31–32
environmental
   cultural   54
   'green' issues   53
   'monitoring'   51–55, 103
   PEST analysis   52–55
EPISTLE analysis   53, 57, 106
European Communication Monitor
      (2009)   2, 11, 162
evaluation   156–78
   benefits of   157–58
   corporate   163–64
   macro model   165
   McDonald's case study
      172–74
   objective measures   168–72
   Olympic Bid case study
      168–72
   principles   160–61
   programme   162
   societal   163
   stakeholder   164

techniques   159–60
terminology   161–62
why practitioners don't   158–60
exhibitions   122, 125

feedback   79
feeling (affective) objectives
      90–91
'feelgood factor'   4
financial relations   123
Financial Times   33
focus groups   65–66, 162
Freedom of Information
      legislation   27
Freeman, R E   23

Gallup   63
games technology   54
Gantt charts   140–41
   example   140
German Public Relations
      Association   159
Golley Slater   128–31
GlaxoSmithKline   74
global warming   1, 53
globalization   1, 55
Gregory, A   12, 163
Greenpeace   101
Grunig, James   100, 101, 102, 103
Guide Dogs for the Blind
      Assocation (GDBA) case
      study   125–27
   audiences   126
   evaluation   127
   key points   127
   objectives   126
   strategy   126
   tactics   126–27

Henslowe, Philip   143

i to i research   169–70
Independent Financial Advisors
      promotion case study   131–34

background 131–33
  key points 133–34
Innocent 4
input 161, 165, 166
internal communication 122
internet, the 55
  communication and 85–86
  groups 66, 103
interviewing 64–65
Ipsos-MORI 55, 63, 163, 169
isolates 84
issues management 55–57

Kincaid, D L 80

Lansons Communications
  121–34
Lerbinger, O 59
'level substitution' 162
leverage points 87
liaison 12
lobbying 122

Macnamara, Jim 165
  micro model of evaluation 166
management by objectives 2
Maslow, A 88
McDonald's case study 172–74
  background 172
  calendar of industry
    events 173–74
  objectives 173
  overview of brand
    positioning 173
measures for evaluation 167–68
  objective 167
  subjective 167–68
media, the 100
  analysis 172–74
  public opinion and 106–07
media campaigns 143
  garden centre chain
    example 144
media relations 122

messages 114–16
  context 115
  crafting 114
  format 115
  presentation 115–16
  repetition 115
  timing 115
  tone 115
  see also communication
Mintel 63, 132
Moss, D A 21
Muslim Council of Britain
  (MCB) 125
mystery shoppers 67

Nationwide Building Society 74
networking 84, 162
'new media' 2
Newman, A 21
news consumption 99–100
Nike 4
Noble, Paul 159

objectives 2
  affective 91
  attitudes/opinions 90–91
  awareness 90
  behaviour 91
  cognitive 90
  conative 91
  evaluation 160
  external constraints 93, 94
  internal constraints 94
  levels 91, 94–96
  organizational 92
  outcome focused 92
  public relations plans and
    92, 95
  quantifiable 93
  research based 92
  reviewing 176
  setting 89–96
  SMART 93
  see also aims

Olympic Bid case study   168–72
  background   168
  importance of evaluation   172
  objectives   169
  segmentation of public
    support   172
opinion leaders   82
opinions   77, 100 *see also* attitudes
organizational analysis   57–59
  culture   57
  prioritizing/linking issues   60
  role of public relations   58
  see also SWOT analysis
organizational characteristics
  30–31
  competitors   30
  employees   31
  mission 30
  nature   31
  sector   30
  size/structure   30
  tradition/history   31
organizational development
  business stage   27–30
  decline   29–30
  growth   28
  maturity   29
  public relations and   25–30
  start-up   28
outcome   161–62, 166
outflow   162
output   161, 165, 166
out-take   161, 165, 166
Oxfam   27

PEST analysis   52–55
Peugeot   114
Pew Research Center   100
Pilkington PLC   36
  corporate public relations
    policy   36–37
planning   35–46, 178
  basic questions   39–41
  comprehensive model   45

  importance of   38–39
  information   38
  objectives   43–44
  process   42
  purpose of   2–5
  review   177
  strategy   39–40
  twelve stages   41–44
  see also evaluation, research,
    strategy
power/interest matrix   104, 105
press conferences   139, 143
press packs   139, 141, 142
programmes, public relations   22,
  109–10
  case studies   125–34, 145–
    49,   168–72, 172–74
  content   110–12
    emotional   112–13
    rational   110–11
  'contact and dialogue'   120–21
  'contract and convince'
    120–21
  dialogue-based campaigns   110
  evaluation   113–14
  information   campaigns   109
  persuasion campaigns   109
  resources   149–55
  sustaining   131
proposition   110–11
  conjecture   111
  'evidence' sources   111–12
  fact   110
  policy   111
  value   111
public opinion   9, 32–33, 99–100
  media and   106–07
public relations   3
  audits   59
  consultancies   153–55
  definition   3
  marketing   14
  organizational functions
    13–16

policy 36–37
position in organizations
    11–16
proportioning effort 108
role in organizations 5–6
strategic role of 3
see also programmes
Public Relations Consultants
    Association (PRCA) 154
public relations department
    16–19, 34
functional structure 17
matrix structure 17–18
resources 34
task-oriented structure 16
public relations professional/
    practitioner 6–11, 149–51
boundary-spanning 8
Chief Risk Manager 32
communication/liaison role 19
communication technician 18
communication manager
    18–19
contextual intelligence 8
contingency planning and 135
media relations 19
position in organization 12
relationship building 7–9
responsibilities 35–36
roles 20
skills 13
publics 23–26, 51, 85, 97–116
active 101
all-issue 101
apathetic 101
aware 101
common to most
    organizations 98
communicating with 102–03
constraint recognition 102
hot-issue 101
latent 101
level of involvement 102
non-publics 101

prioritizing 107–09
problem recognition 102
segmentation techniques
    104–06
single-issue 101
targeting 107
types 100–01

reputation 4–5, 12, 15, 32, 59,
    163
research 47–75, 123
case examples 69–75
    'Snorers Sleep-in' 74–75
    Waste and Resources Action
    Programme (2007)
    69–74
desk 63
embedding in planning
    process 47–49
evaluative 48, 49
focus groups 65–66
formative 48, 50, 97
informal 67–68
internet groups 66
interpreting findings 69
interviewing 65
media 68
monitoring 48, 49
mystery shoppers 67
observation 66-67
one-to-one depth interviews 64-
    65
primary 63-64, 67
programme 48, 49
role of public relations 61-62
secondary 63-64
self-completion questionnaires 64
situation analysis 50
sources of information 63
syndicated surveys 65
telephone interviews 65
tracking surveys 63
see also organizational analysis,
    planning

resources 149–55
  consultancies 153–55
  equipment 152–53
  human 149–51
  operating/materials 151–52
review 157, 174–78
  external drivers 176–77
  internal drivers 177
  strategy and objectives 175–76
Rhone–Poulenc Agriculture
  experiment 56
risk 136–37
  assessment 136–37
    impact 137
    likelihood 137
Rogers, E M 80
Royal Mail 114
Royal Society of Arts 55

Schramm, W 79
segmentation techniques
  104–06
  behaviours 106
  demographics 104, 106
  geography 104
  group membership 104
  media consumption 104
  psychographics 104, 106
  role in decision process 104
  type of power 104
Shannon, C 78
shareholders 105
Sheep Drive Over London Bridge
  case study 145–49
  evaluation 147
  key points 149
  logistics 147–49
  objectives 145
  overview 145
  strategy 146
  target publics 145
Singapore Airlines 54
SMART objectives 93
Smith, R D 110, 111, 112, 113

'Snorers Sleep-in' campaign
  74–75
  background 74
  implementation 74–75
  results 75
  strategy 74
social audits 59–60
social marketing programmes 16,
  105
special events 123
sponsorship 122
stakeholder analysis 59–61
  organizational visibility 59
  organizational reputation 59
stakeholders 2, 9, 23–26, 51
  attitudes 97
  influence/power 25–26
  numbers/location 25
  range 25
stars 84
Steyn, Benita 13
'strategic inflection' 1
strategy 48, 117–20, 143
  communicating 7
  defining 118
  developing 6–7
  levels in organizations 14
  review of 175–76
  tactics and 118, 120
SWOT analysis 58
Sunday Telegraph 167
Sunday Times 167

tactics 118–25
  appropriateness 124
  case studies 125–34
    Guide Dogs for the Blind
      Association 125–27
    Independent Financial
      Advisors 131–34
    The Piper's Trail 128–31
  deliverability 124–25
  range 122–23
  strategy and 118–20

'target groups'   24
task planning techniques
     139–41
   Critical Path Analysis
     141–43
   Gantt Charts   139–41
Technorati   68
The Piper's Trail (Army in
     Scotland) case study
     128–31
   audience   128
   community engagement   129
   educational engagement   129
   evaluation   130–31
   objectives   128
   online PR/website   10
   tactics   128–29
timescales   33, 138–49
   deadlines   138–39
   externally driven   33
   internally driven   33
Trimedia   69
Trimedia Belgium   74–75
Twitter   66

U S Army   23–24
Unbiased.co.uk   131, 122
Uses and Gratification Theory
     87–88

values   2, 57
Vargo guide dog   125–27
viral campaigns   66
Virgin Airlines   54
virtuous circle   4

Waste and Resources Action
     Programme (2007)   69–73
   action (tactics)   71–73
   budget   73
   client objectives   70
   evaluation   73
   key points   73–74
   planning   70–71
   strategy   70
   target audience   70
Watson, Tom   158, 159
Weaver, W   78
web-based communities   84, 103
   bridge-spanners   84
   isolates   84
   liaison role   84
   stars   84
   see also communication,
     networking
White, J   163
Work Foundation, The   55
Worshipful Company of World
     Traders, The   145–49